SOPH ECCLESTONE

Breaking Boundaries in Women's Cricket

BRAVO J. MAX

Copyright © 2024 by Bravo J. Max

All rights reserved. No part of this publication may be reproduced, distributed, or transmitted in any form or by any means, including photocopying or other electronic or mechanical methods, without the prior written permission of the publisher, except in the case of brief quotations embodied in reviews and certain other non-commercial uses permitted by copyright law.

Cover Image Credit

The cover image, "Sophie Ecclestone 2023," is by Stumpsnbails and is licensed under the Creative Commons Attribution-Share Alike 4.0 International license.
Source: Wikimedia Commons (Own work).

DISCLAIMER

This book is an independent publication and is not affiliated with, endorsed, or sponsored by Sophie Ecclestone, the England and Wales Cricket Board (ECB), or any associated organizations. All opinions expressed are those of the author, and quotes are attributed to publicly available sources.

TABLE OF CONTENTS

INTRODUCTION 5
CHAPTER 1 11
EARLY LIFE AND PASSION FOR CRICKET 11
   1.1. Discovering the Love for Cricket 11
   1.2. Family support and early influences 17
   1.3. The Journey through Local Clubs 22
CHAPTER 2
BREAKING INTO PROFESSIONAL CRICKET ... 29
   2.1. Debut for England: A Young Prodigy 29
   2.2. First Experiences in International Matches.. 35
   2.3. Earning a Spot in the Core Team 41
CHAPTER 3 48
ESTABLISHING HERSELF AS A PREMIER SPINNER 48
   3.1. Developing the Spin Magic: Techniques and Training 48
   3.2. Overcoming Challenges and Setbacks 54
   3.3. Becoming a Key Asset in the Team's Bowling Line-Up 60
CHAPTER 4
ACHIEVEMENTS AND MILESTONES 67
   4.1. Record-breaking Performances 67
   4.2. ICC Rankings and Global Recognition 73
   4.3. Awards and Honors in International Cricket. 78
CHAPTER 5 85

SOPHIE'S IMPACT ON WOMEN'S CRICKET..... 85
    5.1. Role in Promoting Women's Cricket in England... 85
    5.2. Inspiring the Next Generation of Cricketers. 91
    5.3. Contributions to Women's Cricket Globally.. 96

CHAPTER 6
THE WOMEN'S ASHES AND WORLD CUP JOURNEYS.. 102
    6.1. Defining Ashes Series Moments............ 102
    6.2. World Cup Appearances and Heroics.... 107
    6.3. Memorable matches and turning points. 115

CHAPTER 7... 123
OFF THE FIELD: PERSONALITY AND PHILOSOPHY... 123
    7.1. The Role Model: Sophie's Influence Beyond the Game... 123
    7.2. Philanthropy and community work......... 128
    7.3. Balancing Life as a Professional Athlete 134

CHAPTER 8
FUTURE ASPIRATIONS AND LEGACY........... 139
    8.1. Goals for the Future............................... 139
    8.2. Sophie's Vision for Women's Cricket..... 144
    8.3. Building a Lasting Legacy...................... 150

APPENDICES... 156
CAREER STATISTICS AND RECORDS............ 156

INTRODUCTION

Being a successful athlete is no picnic; along the way, you'll face obstacles that put your determination, perseverance, and bravery to the test. Sophie Ecclestone has built her career on an unusual combination of natural ability and unwavering determination; her name is now related to women's cricket and the precision, strategy, and refinement with which it is known. As one of the most formidable spinners in modern cricket, her narrative is not just about shattering records but breaking limits that define the fundamental structure of women's cricket.

From the moment Sophie Ecclestone came onto the world stage, she exhibited an incredible maturity much beyond her years. Born in Cheshire, England, in 1999, she began to play cricket at a young age, inspired by her older brother James and supported by a family that saw her talent early on. Even as a teenager, Ecclestone's precision bowling and ability to extract sharp turns made her stand out. She was quickly promoted to the England squad and made her Twenty20 International debut in July 2016 against Pakistan when she was just 17 years old.

After that, she had a meteoric ascent that cemented her place in the sport and helped England become a global leader in women's cricket. Even before she competed in the 2017 Women's World Cup for the first time, Ecclestone was widely considered a top bowler. England's performance in the 2017 ICC Women's Cricket World Cup was memorable, with the squad emerging as champions after a thrilling nine-run triumph over India in the final at Lord's. Even though Sophie was more of a supporting player in this event, she would prove to be a game-changer in later series and tournaments thanks to her impact.

Sophie's most memorable event was the 2020 ICC Women's T20 World Cup in Australia. In a competition that saw her at her peak, she finished as

England's best wicket-taker, collecting eight wickets at an astonishing economy rate of 3.23. Despite the rain-related washout that sent England crashing out of the semi-finals against India, Sophie's mesmerizing performances, such as her pivotal 3 for 7 against Pakistan, showcased her developing talent. She went from being a gifted young player to a seasoned match-winner in the event, someone who could swing the game in her team's favor with a simple pass or shot.

Ecclestone's ability to perform under pressure was further highlighted in the multi-format Women's Ashes series in 2021-22. With England seeking to win the Ashes from a dominating Australian side, Sophie's spells stood out among tight competition. In the one-off Test at Canberra, she bowled a marathon 31 overs in the first innings, securing 3 for 71 and ensuring that England remained in the match. Her unrelenting precision and variations put even the greatest Australian hitters into defensive modes, demonstrating why she had become

England's key weapon in the bowling arsenal. The series, albeit ultimately concluding in Australia's favor, saw Ecclestone emerge as a star performer, finishing with 14 wickets across formats.

The 2022 ICC Women's Cricket World Cup in New Zealand added another chapter to her expanding history. Despite England's shaky start to the competition, Ecclestone's consistency shone through. Her stats of 6 for 36 against South Africa in the semi-final—a career-best—propelled England to the final, where they met Australia. Although England fell short in a high-scoring battle, Sophie's superb tournament numbers of 21 wickets at an average of 15.61 earned her spot as the leading wicket-taker, and she was justifiably included in the Team of the Tournament. As she stood on the podium receiving plaudits, the cricketing world understood that Sophie Ecclestone was no longer merely a potential talent; she was a force to be reckoned with.

Beyond her statistical successes, it is Sophie's manner on the field that sets her apart. Former England captain Charlotte Edwards, herself a classic of the game, recently commented, "Sophie has an innate calmness and a tactical mind that you don't often see in bowlers of her age. She reads the game like a seasoned veteran and always looks a step ahead." Such observations are echoed by her peers and opponents alike, who have consistently praised her for maintaining composure even in high-stakes situations.

Her effect, however, goes beyond statistics and honors. Sophie, a young woman excelling in a sport that has previously been male-dominated, represents a new era of athletes breaking established standards. Her performances have motivated other young girls to take up the sport, believing that they too can play at the highest level. In a sport where spinners are frequently considered supportive bowlers to fast-paced assaults, Ecclestone has revolutionized the role, proving that a spinner can be a match-winner in her own right.

Sophie Ecclestone continues to add chapters to her brilliant career, but her story is far from over. With every wicket she takes, every record she breaks, and every event she dominates, she is not just playing a game—she is constructing a legacy. This book tries to delve into that legacy, chronicling her journey, her accomplishments, and the tenacious spirit that makes Sophie Ecclestone one of the most remarkable figures in the world of cricket today.

CHAPTER 1

EARLY LIFE AND PASSION FOR CRICKET.

1.1. Discovering the Love for Cricket

Sophie Ecclestone's love affair with cricket began long before she joined the international stage. Born on May 6, 1999, in Cheshire, England, Sophie grew up in a family that had a profound enthusiasm for sports. Her early years were defined by an instinctive curiosity and a competitive attitude, attributes that would later define her approach to the game. But, like many young girls in England, Sophie didn't immediately picture herself as a future cricketer. Her passion for the sport was cultivated more informally, as she often found herself joining the neighborhood lads in impromptu matches, playing with improvised stumps and taped tennis balls in local parks.

It was her older brother, James, who originally kindled her interest in the game. James, a keen cricketer himself, had a big influence in Sophie's formative years. He would invite her to practice bowling in the garden or attend local training sessions. At first, Sophie was simply tagging behind, attempting to replicate her brother's tactics, but soon it became evident that she wasn't just a spectator—she was a natural. Her early attempts at bowling were characterized by uncommon precision and an ability to consistently strike a solid length, attributes rare for someone so young. James, noticing her ability, started to challenge her more, often setting up targets or creating different circumstances for her to bowl in. It was during these relaxed yet competitive practices that Sophie's love for cricket flourished, and her goal of one day representing England began to take shape.

Yet, passion alone doesn't guarantee a career in professional athletics. Sophie's family had a vital role in supporting her early dreams. Her parents, Elaine and Paul Ecclestone, were first astonished by Sophie's passion for a sport that, at the time, wasn't as accessible to girls as it is today. However, parents were quick to rally behind her, enrolling her in local groups and making the necessary sacrifices to ensure she had every opportunity to pursue her love. By the time Sophie was 10, she was already playing for the Alvanley Cricket Club's boys' squad, where she held her own against older, stronger players.

Playing in a primarily male setting wasn't without its obstacles. There were times when she had to show herself again and again, not just as a competent player but as a female who belonged in the game. These early experiences of being the only girl on a boys' team honed her competitive edge and tenacity. It also provided her with the tenacity to handle pressure situations, something that would serve her well when she eventually donned the England shirt.

Sophie's brilliance didn't go undetected for long. By the age of 13, she was already on the radar of Cheshire's county coaches, and shortly, she secured a berth in the Cheshire Women's under-15 squad. Her swift progression through the county ranks was a result of her uncompromising work ethic and a fierce resolve to succeed. "Even at that age, she was always striving to be better," remembers her first coach at Cheshire. "She wasn't just interested in getting wickets; she wanted to understand the game, to outthink the batter, to know how to bowl in different conditions. That hunger tore her apart."

It was at this time that Sophie's particular bowling style began to take shape. She began polishing her left-arm orthodox spin under the guidance of skilled trainers, experimenting with different grips and angles. But what made her stand out even more was her ability to retain an astounding amount of control, rarely straying from her line and length. This precision, coupled with her natural turn, gave her a continuous threat. As she began dominating local leagues, it became apparent that Sophie was more than simply a promising player—she was a prodigy in the making.

In 2014, at the age of 15, Sophie's growing career took a huge jump when she was invited to train with the England Women's Development Program. This was her first taste of professional cricket, and though she was younger and less experienced than most of her colleagues, she held her own, impressing the national selectors with her maturity and skill. "She had this remarkable composure," remembers one of her early mentors from the program. "Even when she was up against senior players, she never seemed intimidated. It felt as if she belonged there."

Sophie's exposure to a higher level of competition further spurred her ambitions. It was during this period that she really committed to making cricket her career, juggling school with demanding training regimens and traveling long distances to attend county tournaments. For Sophie, every match, every training session, and every early morning wake-up was a step closer to her ultimate goal—playing for England. Her journey from the backyard matches with her brother to the national setup was a monument to her drive, persistence, and an unyielding trust in her own ability.

This chapter of Sophie Ecclestone's life wasn't only about discovering her love for cricket—it was about discovering who she was as a person. The early obstacles, the sacrifices made by her family, and the lessons acquired on and off the field all contributed to constructing the firm foundation upon which her exceptional career would be built. These critical years were not just about developing as a player, but also about turning a young girl into a future star who would go on to break boundaries and redefine what's possible for women in cricket.

1.2. Family support and early influences

Every athlete's journey begins somewhere, and for Sophie Ecclestone, that path was profoundly anchored in the continuous support of her family. Born into a close-knit household in the tranquil town of Chester, England, Sophie's upbringing was filled with the echoes of family reunions, backyard games, and a spirit of togetherness. It was in this loving environment that Sophie initially discovered her love for cricket—a passion that would be completely accepted and nourished by her family, setting the groundwork for her future success.

Sophie's parents, Elaine and Paul Ecclestone, were not cricketers themselves, but they possessed an astute sense of what it took to foster a desire. They sensed something remarkable in their daughter's early fascination with the game—a spark that went beyond the casual excitement of a young child. For them, it wasn't just about Sophie's skill; it was about providing her the freedom and support to seek what made her truly happy. "We always knew Sophie had a fierce determination in her, but we wanted her to enjoy the game first and foremost," Elaine once stated in an interview, stressing the balance they struck between supporting her dreams and letting her choose her own path.

Sophie's first memories of playing cricket generally involved her older brother, James. James became her first opponent, coach, and mentor, all rolled into one. Whenever they were home after school, the two would spend hours in the garden, transforming the little space into an imaginary cricket ground. With a few stumps propped up against a wall and an old bat in hand, they would re-enact scenarios from their favorite matches, imagining themselves as the stars of the England team. It was during these sessions that Sophie's competitive character finally surfaced. Even though she was younger and less experienced, she always did her best, determined to match James's talent level. As James recounts, "I had to stop taking it lightly on her pretty quickly.

She was determined and wouldn't settle for anything less than getting me out."

What began as sibling rivalry soon morphed into a rigorous training program. James encouraged Sophie to perfect her technique, teaching her the essentials of grip, line, and length while also encouraging her to experiment with spin. Their amicable duels in the backyard became the foundation of Sophie's bowling skill. Over time, what stuck out was her perfect control. Unlike most young bowlers who battled with precision, Sophie could land the ball on a dime over and over again. It was a hint of things to come—a preview of the future star who would bamboozle hitters with her precision and fly.

Recognizing Sophie's burgeoning passion, her parents decided to take the next step. She was enrolled in the Alvanley Cricket Club, a local club known for its youth development initiatives. It was a brave move, considering that Sophie was the lone girl among boys in her age group. But her parents believed that if she was to realize her potential, she needed to confront the hardest competition. At Alvanley, Sophie wasn't treated any differently, and in many ways, that was her benefit. She had to fight for her place, win respect with every delivery, and consistently establish that she was more than capable of holding her own.

At home, Paul and Elaine made sure that Sophie never felt out of place in her pursuit of the sport. Paul, despite a busy work schedule, would take her to games throughout the county, frequently waking up before dawn for long excursions. "It was exhausting at times, but we never questioned it," Paul later shared. "Seeing her smile after a successful game or listening to her talk excitedly about a wicket she took—it made it all worthwhile." Elaine, on the other hand, focused on providing the emotional support that was necessary for a young girl navigating a sport dominated by boys. She would sit through matches, delivering words of encouragement and praising every milestone, no matter how minor.

But probably the most significant influence came not only from her personal family but from the greater cricketing community. Coaches at Alvanley noticed her raw ability and took a keen interest in her growth. They forced her to bowl against older players, improve on her variations, and build a mental toughness that would be important for her future career. One of her early coaches, Mike Guest, says, "Sophie wasn't just another player. She was willing to put in the lengthy yards, bowling for hours on end, and never shying away from critique. You could sense that drive in her eyes."

As Sophie moved through the ranks, the sacrifices made by her family became increasingly obvious. Weekends were no longer about relaxation; they were spent driving to matches, standing by the sidelines in all kinds of weather, and ensuring that Sophie had the best equipment and support. It was a joint effort—a family rallying behind a shared dream. And through it all, they never pressed her; instead, they provided a safety net, telling her that regardless of what occurred on the field, she would always have their undying support.

This familial foundation played a vital role in shaping Sophie's early years. It gave her the confidence to take risks, to embrace challenges, and most importantly, to never doubt her place in the sport she loved. Today, as she stands tall among the world's greatest, Sophie often recalls those early days, attributing her success not just to her own hard work but to the quiet, consistent support of a family that believed in her ability long before anyone else did.

1.3. The Journey through Local Clubs

For Sophie Ecclestone, the transition from a cricket-loving teenager to an internationally known bowler was distinguished by the important developmental years spent in local clubs. It was in these clubs' fostering environment that she began to sharpen her innate talent, learning the complexities of the game and cultivating the competitive spirit that would define her career. Her journey through the local cricket circuits was more than simply a stepping stone; it was the furnace where her skills were molded and her love for the sport developed into an unwavering ambition.

After perfecting her talents in the backyard with her brother James, Sophie's parents made a key choice to enroll her at the Alvanley Cricket Club, a local institution famed for its youth training programs. It was a tremendous step for a little girl who had, up until then, only played informal matches with family and friends. But Alvanley was no ordinary starting point. With a significant focus on cultivating talent from the bottom up, the club offered a disciplined atmosphere where Sophie could go from recreational play to more serious, competitive cricket.

Sophie was the only girl in a sea of boys, but her bowling ability made her stand out. Even at an early age, she demonstrated extraordinary control over her deliveries, routinely landing the ball on a decent length and spinning it sharply. Yet being the only woman on the team wasn't always simple. At times, there were moments of distrust from opponents and even teammates. But Sophie, with her normal drive, never let that stop her. Instead, she utilized these experiences as inspiration, determined to show herself worthy of her seat on the squad. "I remember how some boys would underestimate her," recalls one of her early coaches at Alvanley. "But once she got them out, their perception changed quickly."

As her potential became more clear, Sophie was moved up the ranks, playing in higher age groups and against greater competition. The coaches at Alvanley had a vital influence in this era of her development. They encouraged her to try new variants, polish her flight and tempo, and most importantly, comprehend the mental element of the game. It was here that she began learning how to set up batters, utilizing her deliveries tactically to outthink them rather than merely outplaying them. "It wasn't just about bowling at the stumps," one of her coaches commented. "She started to develop plans, thinking two or three balls ahead, which was remarkable for someone her age."

As Sophie's reputation as a young prodigy spread, she was invited to join the Chester Boughton Hall Cricket Club, a decision that marked a big stride forward in her career. Chester Boughton Hall was a more competitive club, with a rich history of producing top-quality players. Here, Sophie found herself surrounded by players who were equally passionate and skilled, a setting that encouraged her to elevate her game even more. She was no longer only a standout bowler among her classmates; she was now fighting against some of the greatest youth cricketers in the region.

It was at Chester that Sophie finally began to come into her own. She liked the opportunity to train with seasoned players and embraced the challenge of playing against boys who were stronger and more experienced. But instead of being overwhelmed, Sophie thrived. Her performances on the field, including multiple match-winning periods, immediately made her a prominent player in the team's bowling attack. It wasn't long before she began building a reputation for herself beyond the club circuit.

Her performance at Chester drew the attention of county selectors, and Sophie was soon put into the Cheshire women's age-group teams. Competing at the county level provided a whole new set of problems. The caliber of play was higher, and the expectations were greater, but Sophie attacked every match with a calm purpose. Whether it was taking the new ball or being called upon to bowl in pressure circumstances, she thrived on the responsibility, acquiring crucial experience that would serve her well in the years to come.

The critical milestone in her journey through local clubs came when she was selected to represent Cheshire's senior women's squad at barely 14. Playing alongside and against seasoned county players, Sophie's maturity on the field was striking. She was no longer merely a talented young cricketer—she was beginning to display the attributes of a potential star. Her performances for Cheshire eventually led to a call-up to the Lancashire Thunder, the regional women's side competing in the now-defunct Women's Cricket Super League. This opportunity marked her transfer from local clubs to the national level.

Through each of these transitions—from Alvanley to Chester Boughton Hall and eventually to Cheshire and beyond—Sophie's journey was marked by a tireless pursuit of excellence. The local clubs did more than just provide a platform for her progress; they were crucial in defining her understanding of the game, instilling a work ethic, and building the mental toughness needed to win at the top levels. Every session in the nets, every league match, and every wicket taken was a step towards her larger goal of representing England.

Today, when Sophie thinks back at her time spent at these clubs, she acknowledges their influence not just on her game but on her character. The hours spent training on rainy, cold English mornings, the camaraderie enjoyed with colleagues, and the hurdles faced as a young girl participating in a male-dominated sport were all crucial in molding the cricketer—and the person—she is today. Her journey through the local clubs was more than a path to professional cricket; it was the foundation upon which a future legend was constructed.

CHAPTER 2
BREAKING INTO PROFESSIONAL CRICKET

2.1. Debut for England: A Young Prodigy

For any aspiring cricketer, the idea of donning the England jersey is often a faraway aspiration—one that demands years of slogging through the local circuit, polishing talents, and waiting patiently for a crack at the big stage. But for Sophie Ecclestone, her road to the international arena was anything but average. From the moment she was recognized by national selectors as a teenager, her talent and composure marked her apart, establishing her as a prodigy destined for greatness. By the time she made her England debut, Sophie wasn't just a talented teenager; she was a bowler the world was already beginning to notice.

Sophie's ascension to England's senior team was swift, yet well-deserved. After thriving in the England Women's Development Program and continuously outclassing her colleagues at both county and regional levels, she received the call every young cricketer dreams of—an invitation to join the England squad for a series against Pakistan in 2016. At just 17 years old, Sophie was ready to become one of the youngest players ever to represent England in women's cricket. It would have been intimidating for many, but Sophie saw it as the culmination of years of hard work, dedication, and self-confidence.

Her debut occurred on July 3, 2016, in a T20 international against Pakistan at Bristol's County Ground. Stepping onto the field for the first time, clad in England's colors, Sophie's enthusiasm was evident, but so was her determination. Bowling in the shortest format of the game is no simple assignment, especially for a spinner, when the margin for error is limited and the pressure to contain runs is tremendous. Yet Sophie demonstrated a maturity beyond her years. In her four overs, she bowled with precision and control, surrendering just 21 runs and bringing up her maiden wicket by removing Nahida Khan, Pakistan's opener. England won the match handily, chasing down the total of 107 with eight wickets in hand, but it was Sophie's calm and collected bowling that attracted everyone's attention.

Her performance won her a place in the ODI team for the same series when she made her One Day International debut just a few days later in Worcestershire. In a format that needs a balance between aggression and moderation, Sophie once again demonstrated her mettle. She bawled her complete quota of 10 overs, giving away just 42 runs while grabbing the key wicket of Pakistan's captain, Sana Mir, with a brilliantly flighted delivery that confused the veteran batsman. England went on to win the match handily by 212 runs, underscoring their superiority, but Sophie's contribution was important, demonstrating that she was no ordinary debutant.

What set Sophie apart in these early encounters was her daring approach. Despite being surrounded by veteran players, she bowled with the confidence of someone who has been on the international scene for years. "She never looked nervous, not even for a second," her teammate Katherine Brunt later said. "It was as if she knew she belonged out there." This confidence, along with her ability to extract sharp turns even on English grounds famed for favoring seamers, made Sophie an obvious asset for England's bowling attack.

Sophie's first big test came soon after, in the form of a major tournament—the ICC Women's World Cup Qualifiers in early 2017. The tournament was essential for England, not just for qualifying but also as a platform to fine-tune their squad ahead of the main event. Although Sophie wasn't always in the starting lineup, whenever she was called upon, she delivered. Against Sri Lanka, she bowled a tight session, ending with 2 for 22 in 8 overs, helping restrict the opposition to a modest total. England chased down the objective comfortably, but it was Sophie's talent for breaking partnerships that shone out. By the end of the campaign, England had successfully secured their spot in the World Cup, and Sophie's performances had guaranteed her place in the squad.

The largest platform of her young career awaited—the 2017 ICC Women's Cricket World Cup, hosted in England. Although she didn't participate extensively in every game, her presence in the team gave depth and diversity to England's bowling options. The final at Lord's against India was a landmark occasion for women's cricket, bringing a record attendance and millions of fans worldwide. While Sophie didn't get to participate in the final, she remained a vital part of the team's success, rejoicing alongside her teammates as

England clinched a thrilling 9-run victory to lift the World Cup trophy.

Following the World Cup, Sophie became a regular part of England's squad across formats. Her breakthrough year in 2018 saw her seal her position in the T20 side during the ICC Women's T20 World Cup in the Caribbean. In a high-stakes encounter against India, Sophie produced a fantastic session, taking 2 for 22 in four overs, which included the valuable wicket of the dangerous Smriti Mandhana. England sailed to the final, only to be bested by Australia. Despite the defeat, Sophie's efforts throughout the tournament had established her as England's leading spinner, capable of taking on the world's finest hitters and excelling in high-pressure situations.

Sophie's progression from a 17-year-old rookie to a staple in the England team was quick but defined by consistent performances and a maturity that belied her age. Her debut was not simply a moment of personal victory but the beginning of a career that would alter spin bowling in women's cricket. Each game, each wicket, and each tournament since has only underlined what was clear from her very first match—that Sophie Ecclestone was no ordinary prodigy. She was a young star destined to shine brightly, setting new benchmarks for what might be achieved with talent, hard work, and an unshakeable sense of purpose.

2.2. First Experiences in International Matches

Sophie Ecclestone's journey into international cricket was distinguished by her early impact and ability to manage high-pressure situations with a cool manner that belied her age. At just 17 years old, when most teenagers are still balancing school and personal interests, Sophie was competing at the top level, testing her skills against seasoned international players. Her early experiences in international matches were more than just a test of her abilities—they were a revelation of her potential to become one of England's premier bowlers.

Her first taste of international cricket came in the summer of 2016, when she was selected to represent England in a T20I series against Pakistan. Sophie made her debut on July 3, 2016, at Bristol, and the moment she took the ball, it was evident that she was ready for the challenge. Bowling her left-arm orthodox deliveries with precision, she completed a clean spell of 1 for 21 in her four overs, an outstanding accomplishment for any rookie, let alone one so young. In a game noted for its unpredictability and aggressive batting, Sophie's ability to keep a tight economy rate set her apart. England won that match comfortably, chasing down Pakistan's small total of 107 with eight wickets in hand, and although the game itself wasn't tight, it served as an ideal platform for Sophie to demonstrate her talent.

This debut victory won her a berth in the ODI team for the subsequent series against the same opponents. In her One Day International debut, Sophie was entrusted with 10 overs—a testament to the faith the team management had in her ability. Playing at Worcestershire, Sophie bowled with maturity, utilizing her variations expertly against Pakistan's middle order. She picked up her maiden ODI wicket by dismissing Pakistan's captain, Sana Mir, a highly experienced player, with a well-flighted delivery that spun sharply to strike the stumps. Sophie concluded with statistics of 1 for 42, playing a significant role in reducing Pakistan to 165 runs. England's strong batting showing, led by Natalie Sciver and Heather Knight, saw them ease to a 212-run triumph. Sophie's performance in the one-sided match showed she had the temperament and skill to succeed in 50-over cricket.

Sophie's early exposure to international cricket was not restricted to bilateral series. In early 2017, she found herself part of the squad for the ICC

Women's World Cup Qualifiers, held in Sri Lanka. The competition was an important test for England, as they sought to earn their position in the 2018 ICC Women's Cricket World Cup. Sophie's role in the team was still growing, but whenever she was given the opportunity, she succeeded magnificently. In a high-stakes encounter against South Africa, she bowled a disciplined spell of 2 for 28, helping England hold a strong South African squad to 196 runs. England went on to chase the target down handily, and Sophie's contribution to keeping the opposition's total manageable was critical.

The preliminary rounds were a stepping stone for the main tournament later that year—the 2017 ICC Women's Cricket World Cup, hosted by England. Although Sophie didn't participate in every game, her presence in the squad was vital. She was part of the squad rotation scheme, and her performances in the matches she did play proved her ability to step up when it mattered most. In a group-stage match versus the West Indies, Sophie bowled a key spell, handing down just 33 runs in her 10 overs and scooping up the wicket of the explosive Hayley Matthews. England won that match by 92 runs, and the success was critical to preserving their momentum throughout the tournament.

As England progressed to the final, Sophie's role remained primarily supportive, but she took in every moment, learning from her senior teammates and witnessing how they managed the enormous pressure of a home World Cup. The final at Lord's against India was a tense affair, with England narrowly protecting a modest total of 228. Sophie may not have been in the playing XI for that match, but she was there, applauding from the sidelines as England clinched a stunning 9-run victory to lift the World Cup. Being part of that winning squad was a formative experience for Sophie, instilling in her a determination to play a bigger role in England's future campaigns.

The ICC Women's T20 World Cup in 2018 gave Sophie the opportunity to establish herself as a permanent fixture in the team. Held in the Caribbean, the event was a showcase of the world's top T20 talent, and England were hungry to restore their dominance. Sophie stepped up significantly in the group rounds, delivering match-winning performances against top teams. In a must-win game against India, she bowled a stunning stint, getting 2 for 22 in her four overs. Her wickets included the key removal of Smriti Mandhana, one of the game's most destructive hitters. Although England eventually lost to Australia in the final, Sophie's consistency and control throughout the competition were big strengths.

By the end of 2018, Sophie had firmly established herself as a crucial part in England's bowling squad. Her early experiences in international cricket had been defined by a blend of patience, precision, and a natural ability for handling pressure circumstances. She wasn't just a teenage spinner finding her way; she was already a match-winner in her own right. Her performances against nations like Pakistan, South Africa, and India emphasized her ability to adapt to diverse circumstances and formats, indicating that she was not just a talented kid but a bowler who belonged on the world stage.

These formative years established the framework for what was to come—a career that would see Sophie reach to the very top of the ICC rankings and become one of the most feared spinners in women's cricket. Her early experiences were more than just stepping stones; they were the basis of a legacy that would continue to flourish with every wicket taken and every tournament conquered.

2.3. Earning a Spot in the Core Team

Sophie Ecclestone's ascent from a promising young cricketer to a core member of the England Women's Cricket Team is a narrative of determination, talent, and flexibility. As a left-arm orthodox spinner, her journey is marked by an unshakable resolve to achieve her spot among cricket's best, supported by a passionate drive to improve her art. While her debut in international cricket was an exciting start, the shift from a young prodigy to a crucial piece in the team's bowling attack wasn't immediate—it was won through hard effort, consistency, and meaningful performances in high-stakes competitions.

Ecclestone's professional breakthrough came in 2016 when she made her debut for England at the age of 17, but it was in the years that followed that she fully established her spot in the team. After initial exposure to the international circuit, Sophie worked relentlessly to perfect her bowling. She recognized that breaking into the core team wasn't only about displaying promise; it was about producing results regularly on the big stage.

Her success in important competitions like the ICC Women's World Cup and the Women's Ashes was crucial in cementing her spot in the squad. In the 2017 Women's World Cup held in England, Sophie got limited opportunities but made the most of them. In the important group-stage encounter against the West Indies, she took a wicket and demonstrated her trademark economy, keeping the scoring pace down. England went on to win the World Cup, and while Ecclestone wasn't yet a certain starter, the event demonstrated her constant progress. She subsequently recalled, "Watching the team win the World Cup at Lord's was inspiring. I knew then that I had to work even harder to ensure that I could be a significant part of similar occasions in the future" (Ecclestone, as cited in 'The Guardian').

However, it was the 2019 Women's Ashes series that truly confirmed her presence as one of the game's top spinners. The series, contested against Australia, was one of the most fierce fights in modern women's cricket history. Ecclestone's performances were vital in the drawn series, but her display in the Test match, in particular, stood out. In a key moment at Taunton, Ecclestone bowled with remarkable control and maturity far above her years, taking 3 wickets for 30 runs in the first innings, a performance that helped England keep Australia to a manageable score. "She's got the fight of a seasoned veteran," England captain Heather Knight observed of Ecclestone at the time. "What she brings to the table, especially in tight situations, is beyond her age" (Knight, mentioned in 'BBC Sport').

By the time the 2020 ICC Women's T20 World Cup in Australia rolled around, Ecclestone was no longer a peripheral player but a keystone of England's bowling assault. Throughout the competition, she was England's star bowler, consistently among the leading wicket-takers. Her ability to suppress the opposition in the middle overs made a huge difference to England's campaign. Notably, in the group match against Pakistan, she was instrumental in England's 42-run triumph, taking 2 wickets while giving just 12 runs in her four overs—a monument to her economical bowling. Her tremendous consistency earned her a berth in the Team of the Tournament, further establishing her spot in the core squad.

Sophie's approach to winning her place in the team goes beyond match-day results; it's rooted in relentless training and a commitment to expanding her skill set. After England's unfortunate defeat in the semi-finals of the 2020 T20 World Cup, she highlighted her personal resolve to progress as a cricketer. "I want to be the best in the world, and I know that means pushing myself even harder. Every day, I focus on how I can improve my accuracy, my variations, and my reading of the game," she stated in a post-tournament interview ('ESPNcricinfo'). Her passion for self-improvement is evident not only in her tactical improvements, but also in the mental strength she demonstrates during high-pressure situations.

Ecclestone's performances on the world scene were bolstered by her home showings in England. She consistently established herself as one of the most dangerous bowlers in English women's cricket, playing for Lancashire and then for the Manchester Originals in The Hundred. During the debut season of The Hundred in 2021, Sophie emerged as one of the leading wicket-takers, making headlines with her 3 for 21 stint against the Welsh Fire. Her performances throughout the tournament, notably in establishing pressure and restricting run rates, were vital to Manchester United reaching the latter stages of the competition.

What sets Sophie Ecclestone apart is not simply her ability to take wickets, but her exceptional control and economy rate. In an era of fast-paced limited-overs cricket, her bowling is critical to breaking partnerships and exerting pressure on the opposition. She has matured into a bowler who can flourish under pressure, whether it's in a World Cup final or a key Ashes Test match. This maturity, coupled with her developing tactical understanding, ensures that she is not merely a spinner for any given match but a major figure around whom England's bowling schemes are typically formed.

By 2022, Sophie Ecclestone had become one of the most regarded spinners in the world, going to the top of the ICC T20 Bowling Rankings. Her role in the core of England's team was no longer in question—it was an irrefutable reality. She had gone from being a teenager with potential to a global star, earning renown as a player who could turn matches with her brilliance.

As she continues her quest, Sophie remains grounded but driven. In her own words, "I still have so much to achieve. It's about pushing limits, for myself and for the team" ('Sky Sports'). That hunger is what distinguishes Sophie Ecclestone's rise—and why she will be a mainstay in England's core squad for years to come.

CHAPTER 3

ESTABLISHING HERSELF AS A PREMIER SPINNER

3.1. Developing the Spin Magic: Techniques and Training

Sophie Ecclestone's ascent to being one of the leading spinners in international cricket is a monument to her dedication to learning the art of spin bowling. Her trajectory has been distinguished by painstaking technical development, hours of intense training, and a natural love for grasping the nuances of spin. But Sophie's success wasn't merely the product of innate talent—it came from constant refining, hard work, and a dogged devotion to perfecting her trade.

From an early age, Sophie displayed an incredible talent to spin the ball with precision. However, as she moved into professional cricket, she rapidly understood that competing on the world stage required more than simply intrinsic skill. Spin bowling, especially in shorter formats, requires a command of subtle variations, control over flight and trajectory, and a smart cricketing mind to outthink batsmen. Sophie understood this and went on a road of perpetual learning, always seeking to evolve.

One of the main components in her progress was her emphasis on regulating the trajectory and dip of the ball. As a left-arm orthodox spinner, she focuses largely on tricking batsmen by altering the speed and angle of her deliveries. During her early years in England, Sophie trained under the tutelage of instructors who emphasized the importance of control in spin bowling. She spent many hours improving her ability to maintain a consistent line and length while experimenting with slight tempo changes. This combination allowed her to keep batsmen guessing—a technique that would later become one of her defining features.

In an interview with 'The Cricketer', Sophie described her strategy for flighting the ball: "It's all about finding that sweet spot where you can get the batsman to play at the ball but not quite reach it. I love the challenge of setting up a batsman, getting them to think they've got the measure of me, and then slipping in something slightly different." Her understanding of how to manipulate flight and use the crease to create different angles was fundamental in making her one of the most effective spinners on the circuit.

Another crucial component of Sophie's development was her ability to adapt her bowling to changing conditions. Spin bowling, particularly in international situations where pitches can vary considerably, requires a substantial level of adaptation. Sophie's tours in the subcontinent, where pitches tend to provide more turn but also reward those who can control their length, were particularly influential. "Bowling in places like India and Sri Lanka taught me patience. The pitch doesn't always work for you; you have to put the ball in the right place repeatedly "'ESPNcricinfo' interview.

Her time spent playing in Australia's Women's Big Bash League (WBBL) also played a key influence in developing her technique. The faster, bouncier wickets in Australia present a new challenge for spinners, and Sophie had to adjust her method to be effective. She concentrated on drastically altering her speeds and using the crease to her advantage, abilities that ultimately served her well in international contests. "I learned so much from playing in the WBBL. It's one of the best places to test yourself against the world's best players," she remarked, reflecting on her experience.

Sophie's training routine is also worth highlighting as a crucial influence on her progress as a spinner. Unlike quick bowlers, who focus largely on strength and speed, spinners rely on subtlety, endurance, and elegance. Sophie's training generally requires repetition, concentrating on muscle memory to maintain her precision. In addition to this, she spends time focusing on her fitness, ensuring she has the endurance to bowl long spells in Test matches while keeping her intensity. "As a spinner, fitness is crucial. It's not about bowling a short spell, but sustaining pressure over time," Sophie explained in a piece for 'BBC Sport'.

Her ability to flip the ball rapidly while maintaining control is a rare mix, and it's something that sets her apart from many other spinners. Over the years, she has developed a stock delivery—a typical left-arm spinner that drifts away from right-handed batsmen—while also mastering variants like the arm ball, which doesn't spin and catches the hitter off guard. These changes are critical in T20 cricket, as batters typically want to play aggressively. By varying her deliveries, Sophie is able to keep batsmen in check, forcing mistakes and offering wicket-taking opportunities.

Sophie's tactical grasp of the game has also evolved alongside her technical skills. She has developed a smart cricketing brain, often establishing her own fields and working closely with her skipper to outfox opposition batsmen. She has proven particularly excellent at sensing when a batsman is prepared to attack and altering her approach accordingly. "I love the mental side of spin bowling—outthinking the batter, staying one step ahead," she stated in an interview with 'Sky Sports'.

In the end, Sophie Ecclestone's mastery of spin is the culmination of years of hard work, continuous study, and a deep passion for the game. Her progression from a promising adolescent to one of the most feared spinners in world cricket says volumes about her commitment to refining her skills and becoming the best at what she does. With each match, she continues to fine-tune her tactics and challenge herself to new heights, proving that the beauty of spin comes not simply from natural talent but from a lifelong dedication to the art of bowling.

3.2. Overcoming Challenges and Setbacks

Sophie Ecclestone's journey to becoming one of the finest spinners in women's cricket has not been without its struggles and setbacks. While her journey to the top may seem flawless to those who have watched her bowl with unwavering accuracy and control, it has been punctuated by periods of doubt, physical hardship, and the great pressure that comes with the responsibility of being one of the best. However, what sets Sophie apart is her resilience—her ability to take these failures in stride and use them as fuel to improve her game.

At a young age, one of Sophie's earliest problems was dealing with the physical and mental demands of professional cricket. When she made her England debut at barely 17, the expectations placed upon her were great. She was regarded as a youthful prodigy, and while her performances were brilliant, the pressure of being considered the future of England's bowling assault came with its own burdens. Sophie had to swiftly adapt to the pressure of international cricket, juggling the mental stress of regular travel, training, and media attention. Speaking about this moment, Sophie recalls, "It was tough at first. You're young, and you're delighted, but at the same time, everything's happening so fast. I had to learn how to manage the expectations and just focus on my game" ('The Telegraph').

An early setback occurred in the form of injury, a familiar challenge for many elite athletes. In 2017, just as she was starting to establish her position in the England team, Sophie developed a side strain during the Women's Ashes series, forcing her out of the game briefly. Injuries are particularly challenging for bowlers, as they impair rhythm, fitness, and confidence. The injury was a frustrating blow for a spinner like Sophie, whose success relies heavily on tiny motions and exquisite control. "It was hard to sit out, especially in such a big series like the Ashes. I just wanted to be out there helping my team," Sophie stated in an interview with 'BBC Sport'.

The healing process wasn't simple. Aside from the physical recuperation, there was also the emotional obstacle of keeping patient while watching her team compete without her. Yet Sophie used this opportunity to concentrate on her thinking and assess her bowling from a different perspective. Instead of letting the defeat derail her, she watched footage of her bowling and sought guidance from senior players and coaches on how to enhance her variations and game strategy. Her recovery was a monument to her resilience—stronger, more focused, and determined to make up for lost time.

Sophie has had to deal with another important obstacle: the ongoing evolution of women's cricket itself. As the game has gotten more competitive, with more international talent and the rapid emergence of T20 competitions like the Women's Big Bash League (WBBL) and The Hundred, bowlers have had to adjust to faster forms and more aggressive batting. Sophie admitted that responding to these changes was vital to staying relevant at the top level. "Batters are always coming up with new shots, new ways to score runs. As a bowler, you must evolve with the game. If you don't, you'll get left behind," she remarked in an interview with 'ESPNcricinfo'.

Facing power-hitters in T20s, Sophie had to concentrate on her variations and learn how to outsmart batters who were always ready to attack. She began experimenting more with her pace, incorporating more subtle adjustments in flight and direction to fool the opposition. This wasn't just a physical adjustment but a mental one. Sophie had to remain confident even when hitters took risks against her, knowing that a spinner's success typically rested in patience and perseverance. This mental resilience helped her remain collected, even in the face of onslaughts from aggressive hitters in T20 leagues around the world.

Perhaps one of Sophie's biggest obstacles is reconciling her professional cricket life with her personal life. Sophie, a young woman in her early twenties, has had to negotiate the responsibilities of being a high-profile athlete while still trying to preserve some sort of normalcy. The demanding schedule of international cricket, with tours and tournaments often taking her away from home for months, has meant missing out on significant moments with family and friends. In an interview with 'Sky Sports', Sophie revealed that homesickness had been one of her major struggles early in her career. "I love what I do, but it's challenging being away from home for so long. You miss birthdays, weddings, and things like that. It's tough, but I've learned how to cope," she said.

To overcome this, Sophie has created a solid support structure, both inside the team and back home. Her family's steadfast support has been vital, and the camaraderie within the England team has helped her cope with the stress of international cricket. Additionally, she has worked with sports psychologists to create mental skills for handling the stress of professional athletics, specifically focusing on mindfulness and staying present during challenging moments on the pitch.

Through all these challenges—injuries, pressure, new formats, and personal sacrifices—Sophie Ecclestone has not only persisted but thrived. Each setback has been an opportunity for growth, and each struggle has fueled her drive to be the best. Her capacity to meet hardship head-on and emerge stronger is what actually identifies her as one of the world's finest spinners. In her own words, "Every setback is just another step toward success. It's about pushing through and showing to yourself that you can conquer anything" ('The Guardian').

3.3. Becoming a Key Asset in the Team's Bowling Line-Up

Sophie Ecclestone's transformation from a bright prospect to a vital figure in England's bowling assault has been nothing short of extraordinary. Over the years, she has matured into a major weapon in the team's bowling line-up, constantly producing under duress and becoming the bowler her teammates and captains turn to in important moments. What makes Sophie a vital member of the squad is not just her outstanding numbers but also her ability to understand the game, keep composure, and alter her bowling to suit any situation.

One of the defining qualities of Sophie's growth has been her ability to execute with accuracy, particularly in limited-overs formats like One Day Internationals (ODIs) and T20s. As a left-arm orthodox spinner, her job in England's bowling line-up has typically been to manage the middle overs, providing pressure by restricting runs and creating possibilities for wickets. This technique was especially on display during the 2020 ICC Women's T20 World Cup, where Sophie was England's standout bowler. She was England's go-to player throughout the tournament, breaking partnerships and delaying opponent run rates. Her outstanding economy rate, consistently under six runs per over, along with her penchant for getting key wickets, reinforced her reputation as a match-winner.

Her capacity to execute in high-pressure situations is one of the reasons she has become such a valuable member of the team. In T20 cricket, where every ball can alter the tide of a match, Sophie's cool manner and constant accuracy have often proved the difference between victory and failure for England. "Sophie's always the one you want to turn to when you need control and a breakthrough," captain Heather Knight once observed, highlighting Ecclestone's crucial role in the team. "She doesn't just bowl well; she leads our attack with intelligence and maturity beyond her years" (Knight, quoted in 'BBC Sport').

One of the crucial instances that demonstrated Sophie's growing relevance in England's bowling line-up came during the 2019 Women's Ashes series. England faced Australia, the most dominant side in women's cricket at the time, and needed something exceptional to challenge their fierce rivals. Sophie stepped up, providing one of her most memorable performances during the Test match at Taunton. Her 3-for-30 in the first inning was a masterpiece of controlled spin bowling. Sophie constantly probed the Australian batsmen, exploiting every hint of turn and keeping the scoring rate in check. Although the series finished in a draw, Sophie's performance firmly confirmed her as England's elite bowler, capable of taking on the world's finest.

What sets Sophie apart is her versatility. While some spinners struggle to alter their style between formats, Sophie has perfected the skill of switching gears depending on the match situation. In Test matches, she bowls with patience, employing the extra time and longer periods to wear out batsmen. In contrast, her T20 bowling is all about variation—mixing up her pace, flight, and angles to keep batters guessing. "It's about reading the game and knowing what the team needs from you at any moment," Sophie stated in an interview with 'ESPNcricinfo'. "Sometimes it's about taking wickets; other times it's about stopping the flow of runs. Being able to adapt fast is what makes you useful to the team."

Her ability to read the game is a vital aspect of her success. As Sophie has gained experience, she has developed a smart cricketing intellect, often establishing her own fields and working closely with the captain to design game strategies. "Sophie has an innate understanding of how to break down batters," observed former England coach Mark Robinson. "She doesn't just bowl a good ball; she builds over after over, setting traps and executing them with pinpoint accuracy" ('The Telegraph'). This cricketing intellect has made her one of the leaders in England's bowling squad, even at a relatively young age.

Beyond her particular skill, Sophie's involvement in the squad extends to teaching younger players. Having gone through the ranks herself, she understands the challenges new players feel when breaking into international cricket. She has embraced the responsibility of mentoring the next generation of spinners, offering advice and assistance to those going through the England system. Her participation in the squad is not only a prominent wicket-taker, but also a role model for others. "Sophie's influence in the dressing room is huge," remarked teammate Tammy Beaumont in an interview with 'Sky Sports'. "She's always the first to lend a hand or give advice, and she leads by example on the field."

Sophie Ecclestone had become not only a significant asset in England's bowling line-up as of 2022, but also one of the most feared spinners in international cricket. Her consistency across all formats, her ability to execute in high-pressure situations, and her ever-growing cricketing IQ have confirmed her as a major player in England's bowling attack. Whether it's a Test match, ODI, or T20, Sophie's contributions are crucial, and she continues to be the player her teammates rely on when the going gets tough.

With her blend of skill, knowledge, and leadership, Sophie has become much more than a talented bowler. She has matured into a linchpin of England's bowling squad, a player whose presence gives the team an edge in every competition. In

Sophie's own words, "I want to be the best version of myself for the team. That's what drives me, knowing I can give when it counts most" ('The Guardian'). Her ability to do just that is what makes her one of the world's most valuable players today.

CHAPTER 4
ACHIEVEMENTS AND MILESTONES

4.1. Record-breaking Performances

Sophie Ecclestone's career is already replete with incredible exploits and record-breaking performances, making her one of the most famous characters in women's cricket. Her gradual ascent as an extraordinary bowler has helped her not only cement her spot in the England team but also smash records that have propelled her to global fame. With each milestone, Sophie has demonstrated that she's not simply a steady performer but a trailblazer in women's cricket.

One of the defining records in Sophie's career is her climb to the top of the ICC T20I Bowling Rankings. In March 2020, at just 20 years old, Sophie became the number one-ranked T20 bowler in the world after an incredible run of performances in the ICC Women's T20 World Cup. Her climb to the top wasn't just a brief moment; it was the culmination of years of hard work and dedication to her trade. Throughout the competition, Sophie displayed her ability to dominate the middle overs, restricting the opponent with her controlled spin. She finished the competition as the second-highest wicket-taker, taking 8 wickets at an exceptional economy rate of 3.23. Her finest figures came against the West Indies, where she took 3 wickets for 7 runs, showcasing her talent for breaking partnerships on vital occasions.

Reflecting on the feat, Sophie acknowledged the significance of reaching the peak of the rankings but stayed grounded. "It's an amazing feeling to be ranked number one, but I'm always looking to improve. For me, it's about consistency and continuing to challenge myself against the greatest players in the world," she said in an interview with

'Sky Sports'. This milestone solidified Sophie's standing as a world-class spinner, but it also signaled the beginning of a time where she would go on to set many more records.

Sophie's dominance in T20 cricket has been paralleled by her performance in the One Day International (ODI) format. In 2021, she achieved the astounding record of becoming the fastest England player to reach 50 wickets in T20Is. She attained this milestone in just 34 matches, shattering the previous record held by Anya Shrubsole. This record speaks volumes about her effect in the shortest format of the game, where the pressure is frequently at its highest and bowlers need to perform in short spells. Her economical bowling and wicket-taking abilities combine to make her one of England's most valuable assets in T20 cricket.

One of her most remarkable individual performances came during the 2022 ICC Women's Cricket World Cup. In the semi-final against South

Africa, Sophie unleashed a spell of bowling that will be remembered as one of the greatest in World Cup history. She got 6 wickets for just 36 runs, the greatest bowling performance by an Englishwoman in a World Cup semi-final. Her stint utterly decimated the South African batting line-up and sealed England's spot in the final. This performance not only smashed records but also highlighted Sophie's ability to step up in the most high-pressure situations. England's head coach, Lisa Keightley, lauded her performance, stating, "Sophie's spell was nothing short of magical. It's the kind of bowling performance that wins you World Cups, and she delivered when the team needed it most" ('BBC Sport').

Another notable milestone came in the Women's Ashes series, where Sophie became one of the youngest English players to take five wickets in an innings during a Test match. In the 2022 Ashes Test at Canberra, Sophie took 5 for 94 in Australia's first innings, a performance that helped England compete against one of the strongest sides in women's cricket. Her ability to capture a five-wicket haul in the longest format of the game, where patience and technique are critical, further demonstrated her versatility as a bowler across all formats.

Sophie's achievements extend beyond individual milestones to those that reflect her consistency and durability in the game. By 2022, she had become the first woman in England's history to hold the number one slot in both the ICC T20I and ODI bowling rankings simultaneously, a testament to her consistent performance across all formats. This performance is particularly impressive given the contrasting skill sets required to excel in both formats—T20 cricket needs rapid thinking and the capacity to adapt, while ODI cricket rewards consistency and endurance.

Beyond the numbers, Sophie's record-breaking achievements have contributed to England's success on the international scene. Whether it's her match-winning stints in World Cups, her important part in the Ashes, or her dominance in bilateral series, Sophie's capacity to deliver game-changing moments has been pivotal in England's successes. She has consistently performed when the stakes are highest, a skill that separates the great players from the excellent.

As she continues to break records and create new milestones, Sophie remains focused on what lies ahead. "Records are great, but for me, it's about winning games for England and contributing to the team's success. That's what drives me every day," she said in an interview with 'The Telegraph'. With her remarkable talent, unmatched work ethic, and ability to rise to the occasion, Sophie Ecclestone is not only rewriting the record books but also molding the future of women's cricket.

4.2. ICC Rankings and Global Recognition

Sophie Ecclestone's rise to global cricketing fame is mirrored not just in her accomplishments on the field but in her persistent dominance of the ICC rankings, which have entrenched her place as one of the top bowlers in the world. From her early days as a brilliant adolescent to becoming the top-ranked bowler in international cricket, Sophie's journey has been marked by a series of milestones that highlight her outstanding ability and unmatched consistency. Her constant ascension through the ICC rankings is a credit to her hard work, versatility, and ambition to succeed at the highest level.

One of the most significant successes in Sophie's career came in March 2020, when she became the number one-ranked T20I bowler in the world. At just 20 years old, Sophie's ascension to the top of the ICC T20I bowling rankings was a reflection of her dominance in the shortest version of the game.

Her ability to restrict runs and capture critical wickets made her a standout performer in the ICC Women's T20 World Cup 2020, where she played a key role in England's progress to the semi-finals. Her efforts throughout the competition were nothing short of extraordinary, with an economy rate of just 3.23, demonstrating her control and precision. She was England's go-to bowler during the middle overs, continuously exerting pressure on the opposition and forcing mistakes from even the most experienced players.

Reflecting on her achievement, Sophie remained humble despite the global recognition. "It's a great feeling to be ranked number one, but for me, it's all about helping the team win games," she stated in an interview with 'Sky Sports'. Her concentration on contributing to the team's success rather than individual accolades is a characteristic of her character, and it is this selflessness that has endeared her to fans and teammates alike.

Sophie's rise to the top of the ICC rankings didn't stop with T20 cricket. In 2021, she acquired the unique distinction of being rated number one in both T20I and ODI bowling rankings concurrently, being the first English woman to hold this title. This dual dominance across forms emphasized her versatility as a bowler and her ability to react to varied match scenarios. In the 50-over game, when bowlers are needed to sustain pressure over longer durations, Sophie's accuracy and variations made her one of the most feared bowlers in the world. Her ability to maintain an economy rate while routinely taking wickets meant that she was a continuous threat in ODI cricket.

Sophie's recognition at the global level extends far beyond rankings. She has been named in many ICC Teams of the Year, an acknowledgment of her impact on the world scene. In 2020, she was named in the ICC Women's T20I Team of the Year, a testament to her exceptional efforts in the T20 format. The following year, in 2021, Sophie was again honored when she was named in the ICC Women's ODI Team of the Year, cementing her status as one of the finest bowlers in both formats. These honors are a measure of her constancy and the respect she commands from the international cricketing community.

Her peers, too, have been vociferous about Sophie's impact on the global stage. Former Australian captain Meg Lanning recently stated, "Sophie's ability to control the game with the ball is something we really respect. She's one of those bowlers who can transform a match with only a couple of overs" ('The Guardian'). High praise from a player of Lanning's stature speaks loudly about Sophie's standing among the world's best.

In addition to her performances for England, Sophie's experiences in domestic leagues around the world have also won her outstanding reputation. Playing in the Women's Big Bash League (WBBL) and The Hundred, Sophie has constantly been among the best performances, further strengthening her worldwide image. Her supremacy in these tournaments, where she has often been one of the leading wicket-takers, has helped her earn a reputation far beyond England. As a prominent player in The Hundred, Sophie's role as the spearhead of Manchester Originals' bowling attack highlighted her ability to inspire and lead both by example and performance.

Sophie's achievements in the ICC rankings are even more remarkable because she has done so much at such a young age. While many players spend years working their way up the ranks, Sophie's inherent talent, along with her diligence ethic, has helped her to reach the top while still in her early twenties. But despite her early success, Sophie remains focused on the future, continually looking for ways to enhance and grow her game. In an interview with 'BBC Sport', she remarked, "It's great to be recognized, but there's always more to achieve. I want to keep getting better and help England win more games and tournaments."

Sophie's regular presence at the top of the ICC rankings and global notoriety are not only a reflection of her own skill, but also of her value to the England squad. Whether it's in the high-pressure conditions of World Cups or bilateral series, Sophie's ability to deliver time and time again makes her a valuable asset for her team. As she continues to smash records and achieve new milestones, Sophie Ecclestone is not only establishing her own legacy but also pushing the frontiers of what is possible in women's cricket on the global arena.

4.3. Awards and Honors in International Cricket

Sophie Ecclestone's career has been highlighted by several trophies and distinctions, recognizing her great contributions to international cricket. She has received acclaim as one of the most consistent and dominant bowlers in the world, not just for her on-field exploits but also for her influence on the global scene. From being named in elite ICC teams to winning honors that acknowledge her unrivaled skill and impact, Sophie's trophy cabinet has steadily filled up with awards that represent her ascent to the top of the cricketing world.

Sophie was named the ICC Women's Emerging Player of the Year in 2018, which was one of the most notable accolades she received. At just 19 years old, this trophy was a signal to the cricketing world that Sophie was not merely an emerging star but a player who had already made her imprint on the international arena. The accolade came after several strong performances, particularly in the ICC Women's World T20 and bilateral series, where she established herself as a dependable wicket-taker for England. This accolade underlined her capacity to succeed at the top level despite her young age, setting the scene for even greater achievement in the years to come.

In 2020, Sophie's dominance in T20 cricket was further recognized as she was named in the ICC Women's T20I Team of the Year. This distinction came after a succession of match-winning performances, including her remarkable period in the ICC Women's T20 World Cup. Throughout the tournament, Sophie was England's star bowler, constantly providing economical spells and scooping up big wickets at crucial occasions. Her control, variety, and ability to bowl under duress made her a vital addition for the team. Being chosen for the ICC T20I Team of the Year was a testament to her consistency and brilliance in the shortest version of the game. Sophie graciously accepted the recognition, adding in an interview with 'Sky Sports', "It's always an honor to be recognized, but for me, it's about playing my role in the team and helping us win matches."

Her recognition didn't stop with T20 cricket. In 2021, Sophie was named in the ICC Women's ODI Team of the Year, an acknowledgment of her versatility and supremacy across formats. This prize was particularly noteworthy as it showed her ability to excel in the longer formats, where persistent pressure and consistency are key. Throughout the year, Sophie had been England's go-to bowler in ODIs, often breaking partnerships and suppressing opposition batters with her accurate and cunning spin bowling. Her participation in the ICC ODI Team of the Year further reinforced her standing as one of the top bowlers in the world, regardless of the format.

Sophie's efforts were also recognized on the home front, with many domestic prizes noting her contributions to English cricket. In 2021, she was awarded the England Women's Player of the Year by the England and Wales Cricket Board (ECB). This award honored Sophie's consistent accomplishments in both international and domestic cricket, particularly her leadership in the bowling department. Her contribution in the Women's Ashes series, when she played a significant part in holding Australia to competitive totals, and her spectacular performances in The Hundred with the Manchester Originals made her an ideal candidate for the prize. Reflecting on the honor, Sophie remarked, "It's been a great year, and to be recognized like this means a lot to me. I'm just focused on continuing to grow and contributing to the team's success" ('BBC Sport').

Another big milestone in Sophie's career came in 2022 when she was selected the ICC Women's Cricketer of the Month for May. This award followed her remarkable efforts in a bilateral series against South Africa, where she took critical wickets across formats and played a vital part in England's triumphs. The monthly award, established to reward excellent performances in international cricket, was a testament to Sophie's ability to perform consistently across all formats and against some of the finest teams in the world.

Sophie's presence on the global scene has also led to her being a part of many ICC Teams of the Decade and garnering distinctions from cricketing authorities worldwide. Her dominance in worldwide tournaments like the Women's Big Bash League (WBBL) and The Hundred has further strengthened her international prominence, resulting in accolades that extend beyond England and the ICC. These include multiple "Player of the Match" accolades in domestic and international championships, reflecting her ability to influence the course of matches with her bowling.

While medals and distinctions are a reflection of her talent and contributions, Sophie has always stayed grounded in her approach. In interviews, she constantly emphasizes that individual praise is secondary to team accomplishment. "It's always nice to get awards, but I play for my team. If I can help England win matches and tournaments, that's what counts most to me," she said in a candid interview with 'The Guardian'. This humility, coupled with her constant quest to improve, makes her a role model for budding cricketers around the world.

As Sophie Ecclestone continues to break records and spearhead England's bowling attack, it is apparent that her list of trophies and distinctions will only continue to expand. Her ability to produce on the greatest stages, along with her work ethic and passion for the sport, assures that she will remain one of the most celebrated players in women's cricket for years to come.

CHAPTER 5

SOPHIE'S IMPACT ON WOMEN'S CRICKET

5.1. Role in Promoting Women's Cricket in England

Sophie Ecclestone's impact on women's cricket extends far beyond her record-breaking performances and individual awards. As one of England's most prominent players, she has become a significant figure in promoting and growing the profile of women's cricket across the country. Sophie's on-field success, leadership, and visibility have helped inspire a new generation of young girls to take up the sport, breaking down barriers and making cricket more accessible and appealing to a wider audience. Her influence has helped to the rapid growth of women's cricket in England, at both the grassroots and professional levels.

From the outset of her career, Sophie has been a role model for young ladies hoping to play cricket. When she broke onto the scene as a teenager, she gave a fresh face in a sport that had long been dominated by male personalities in England. Her story—of a young girl from Cheshire who aspired to become one of the world's top bowlers—resonated with many. The fact that she hit the international scene at barely 17, with an unpretentious approach and a calm confidence, made her relatable and encouraging. Sophie's success at an early age communicated to many aspiring cricketers that with considerable effort, dedication, and enthusiasm, it was feasible to compete at the highest levels.

Her role in promoting women's cricket evolved alongside the sport's evolution in England. Over the past decade, women's cricket has garnered significant attention, thanks in part to high-profile tournaments such as the ICC Women's World Cup and the development of professional domestic leagues like The Hundred. Sophie's performances as one of the stars of these contests have attracted a new audience to the women's game, creating excitement and media attention that hadn't existed in previous years. Her spectacular displays in World Cups and Ashes series, in particular, have played a big influence in boosting the awareness of women's cricket.

One of Sophie's most significant contributions to promoting the sport occurred in 2021 with the establishment of The Hundred, a unique new competition aimed at appealing to younger audiences and families. Sophie, a marquee player for the Manchester Originals, became one of the tournament's faces. Her appearance as one of the standout players in a high-profile, extensively broadcast competition helped push attention to the women's game at a level that had rarely been seen before. "The Hundred has been brilliant for women's cricket," Sophie stated in an interview with 'Sky Sports'. "It's brought a whole new audience to the game, and you can see how many more young girls are getting involved because of it."

Her involvement in The Hundred was not just about playing on the field; it was also about promoting the competition off it. Sophie was highly involved in media appearances, interviews, and promotional efforts for the competition, utilizing her position to encourage more young females to take an interest in cricket. Her relaxed, personable personality made her a favorite with fans, and her eagerness to engage with young cricketers—whether through school visits, social media engagements, or community events—cemented her role as a vital ambassador for the sport.

Sophie's impact on promoting women's cricket isn't confined to her public appearances or media activities. On a personal level, she has taken on a mentorship role within the England team, helping to guide younger players and support those entering the international setup. Sophie, a young player who herself benefited from the guidance and support of veteran players, has been anxious to pass on her expertise and help the next generation of cricketers flourish. This leadership, both on and off the field, has increased the sense of community within English women's cricket and established a culture of support and encouragement that benefits the sport as a whole.

In addition to her mentorship position, Sophie has been an ardent champion for greater funding in women's cricket. She has frequently stressed the need for greater financing, better facilities, and increased media coverage to help the game continue to flourish. Her profile as one of the world's top cricketers has allowed her to speak out on these concerns, fighting for equality and reforms that will benefit future generations of players. "We've come a long way, but there's still a lot more to be done," Sophie stated in an interview with 'The Guardian'. "We need to keep pushing for more opportunities for women in cricket, whether that's through better facilities, more professional contracts, or more exposure for the game."

Sophie's significance in developing women's cricket in England cannot be emphasized. She has played a significant role in revolutionizing the sport and encouraging a new generation of female cricketers through her performances, visibility, and activism. As a role model, she continues to break down boundaries, encouraging young girls to dream big and showing them that they can achieve success in a sport that was once believed out of reach. Her accomplishments, both on and off the field, have helped lift women's cricket to new heights in England, and her impact will be felt for years to come as more young girls pick up a bat or ball, inspired by Sophie Ecclestone's journey.

5.2. Inspiring the Next Generation of Cricketers

Sophie Ecclestone has become a significant character in the evolution of women's cricket, encouraging young cricketers across the world with her extraordinary skill, dedication, and tireless passion for the game. From the moment she debuted for England, Sophie has symbolized the zenith of what hard work and persistence can achieve. More than just her successes on the field, however, it is the way Sophie has carried herself, both as a player and a role model, that has made her a beacon of inspiration for the next generation of cricketers.

Sophie Ecclestone's composure and maturity on the pitch are two of her most distinguishing characteristics. Despite her early age when she got into the England squad, Sophie immediately garnered the respect of her teammates and opponents. This trait, together with her record-breaking performances, made her a figure to admire for aspiring players. Young players who may have been intimidated by the high pace and competitive nature of international cricket found a role model in Sophie, who stayed grounded and cool under pressure. Reflecting on her trip, Sophie once said, "'I've always tried to stay calm in the middle, no matter what the situation is. That's when you can think clearly and make the appropriate decisions." (BBC Sport). It's this kind of thinking that young cricketers look up to, realizing that beyond talent, success in cricket demands mental fortitude and resilience.

Sophie's route to achievement also speaks eloquently about the value of determination. She was part of a generation that saw a tremendous transformation in the opportunities available to women in cricket. Growing up, Sophie didn't always have access to the same resources or visibility as her male colleagues. Yet she persisted, polishing her talents through local clubs and finally gaining a berth in the England squad. Her climb to the top has shown young girls that they can dream big and overcome the hurdles that previously limited women in sports. In an interview with 'Sky Sports', Sophie commented, "'There's no reason why any girl can't make it to the highest level now. The opportunities are there, and if you work hard enough, you can do anything.'" This message has resonated with countless young players who see her as proof that hard work, paired with passion, can open doors once thought closed.

What further sets Sophie apart is her persistent commitment to give back to the cricketing community. Whether through her involvement in youth development initiatives or her open advice to fledgling cricketers, Sophie has always stressed encouraging the next generation. She routinely participates in coaching clinics, sharing not only her technical expertise but also her experiences as a young woman finding her way in a male-dominated sport. Many who have attended these sessions remark on Sophie's personable attitude and genuine desire to help others achieve. After meeting her, a youth cricketer once claimed, "Sophie made me feel like I could do anything. She didn't just talk about cricket but about believing in yourself and enjoying the game."

Her role as an ambassador for women's cricket extends beyond England. Sophie's success in the game has lifted her to a global platform where her actions and words carry considerable weight. As women's cricket continues to rise in prominence, Sophie's exploits in international competitions, such as the Women's Ashes and ICC tournaments, have gained worldwide attention, prompting interest and adoration from young players across many countries. Through social media and her performances on international stages, Sophie has become a symbol of brilliance and perseverance, inspiring girls from various backgrounds to pick up a bat or a ball and pursue their aspirations in cricket.

It's also crucial to notice how Sophie's success has coincided with the greater movement of growing awareness and recognition for women's sports. Sophie's name has grown, as has the exposure of women's cricket to mainstream viewers. This increasing prominence not only motivates new cricketers but also pushes society to embrace the idea of women's sports being just as competitive, entertaining, and skillful as men's. Sophie, as a key character in this shift, has not only inspired future players but also played a role in redefining perceptions of women in sports.

Inspiration for the next generation of cricketers isn't only about performing well on the field, and Sophie Ecclestone understands that. It's about showing that the road to success is filled with hurdles, but those challenges can be conquered with commitment, hard work, and passion. It's about being approachable and giving your time, as Sophie is, in helping younger athletes understand that they too can achieve greatness. And most importantly, it's about carrying the torch for women's cricket, ensuring that the opportunities available today continue to expand for future generations.

5.3. Contributions to Women's Cricket Globally

Sophie Ecclestone's effect on women's cricket reaches far beyond the bounds of England. Her impact is global, changing the way women's cricket is regarded and played around the world. Sophie, one of the major characters in modern cricket, has contributed to the development of the sport through her extraordinary performances, her prominence as an ambassador, and her efforts to support inclusivity and progress in women's cricket on a global scale.

Sophie's regular top-tier performances are one of the most significant ways she has contributed to the world game. From game Cups to the Women's

Ashes, Sophie has established herself time and again as one of the most formidable spinners in the game. Her supremacy with the ball, whether in T20s or Tests, has garnered her international notoriety and secured her place as one of the game's elite bowlers. In doing so, she has set the bar for what is expected of cricketers in the women's game, inspiring players from all corners of the world to better their talents and match her level of perfection.

As a teenage cricketer coming into the England squad, Sophie had little clue how quickly her performances would gain global attention. Reflecting on her early days, she stated, "'I just wanted to play for England, but when you start seeing the way people look up to you, especially girls from other countries, it hits you that you're part of something bigger'" (The Guardian). Through her successes, Sophie has become a figure that cricketers from countries like Australia, India, South Africa, and New Zealand look up to. Her ability to transcend national boundaries has given her a unique platform to impact women's cricket globally, not only as a player but as a symbol of what women's cricket can achieve on the world stage.

Sophie's contribution to the evolution of women's cricket globally obviously goes beyond her on-field skills. She has been an advocate for greater investment in the women's game, particularly in nations where the sport is still emerging. In interviews and public appearances, Sophie has continually asked for greater money, better facilities, and increased media coverage to help the sport flourish globally. Speaking to 'The Independent', she emphasized, "'Women's cricket has so much potential, but we need to keep pushing for equal opportunities, especially in countries where girls still don't have the same support.'" This advocacy is crucial in countries where women's cricket is often overshadowed by men's, and it is through players like Sophie that these issues gain the attention they deserve.

Furthermore, Sophie's participation in global leagues, such as the Women's Big Bash League (WBBL) in Australia and The Hundred in England, has played a crucial role in presenting her talent to foreign audiences. These leagues, which feature players from across the globe, offer a platform for women's cricket to grow and adapt via cross-cultural exchanges of skill and experience. Sophie's participation in these leagues has brought attention not only to her particular brilliance but also to the greater story of women's cricket being a competitive, entertaining sport. Her success in these leagues has proved that women's cricket is no longer bound to national lines; it is a genuinely global game.

Sophie's contributions are also seen through her work with young cricketers worldwide. Whether it's through mentoring programs, overseas tours, or her participation at global cricketing events, Sophie has continually been a figure of inspiration and guidance. Young players from rising cricketing nations, such as Thailand, Bangladesh, and the West Indies, have drawn inspiration from her path. Sophie frequently discusses the importance of fostering talent globally and the need to create a more inclusive environment for women in cricket. In one interview, she commented, "'I love seeing girls from all over the world picking up a bat or ball. It's exciting to think that we're creating a future where girls everywhere feel like they belong in cricket." (Sky Sports).

Additionally, her influence extends into the world of representation. Sophie Ecclestone has become one of the faces of women's cricket in the media, promoting the game and striving for wider visibility. In many ways, her global presence has helped transform perceptions of women's cricket, not only as a niche sport but as a serious, professional operation that requires attention. Sophie, one of the world's top-ranked bowlers, has become a symbol of excellence and a champion for the continued growth of the game.

In conclusion, Sophie Ecclestone's contributions to women's cricket globally are significant and complex. Her performances on the field have encouraged other young cricketers to chase their aspirations, while her advocacy off the field has helped push for the essential adjustments to create a more equal and inclusive sport. As the women's game continues to flourish worldwide, Sophie's significance in establishing this new era of cricket cannot be emphasized. Through her skill, enthusiasm, and leadership, she has made an indelible impression on the global cricketing landscape, guaranteeing that future generations will have the opportunity to excel on the world stage.

CHAPTER 6
THE WOMEN'S ASHES AND WORLD CUP JOURNEYS

6.1. Defining Ashes Series Moments

Sophie Ecclestone's journey in the Women's Ashes has been nothing short of incredible, filled with defining moments that have shown her extraordinary skill, resilience, and game-changing abilities. The Women's Ashes—a fiercely contested series between England and Australia—has historically been a stage where some of the finest cricketing talents emerge, and Sophie has repeatedly proven herself to be one of the major participants in this rivalry. Her contributions to these high-stakes matches have not only helped shape her personal legacy but also made a huge impact on England's performances in this famous series.

One of Sophie's initial defining moments in the Ashes came during the 2019 series. At barely 20 years old, she was already being relied upon as England's frontline spinner—a rare feat for such a young athlete. The pressure of performing against Australia, one of the most powerful teams in women's cricket, could have been overpowering for anyone, but Sophie flourished under it. In the Test match at Taunton, she delivered one of her spectacular performances, collecting important wickets in the first innings to keep Australia's powerful batting lineup in check. Her control, fly, and guile were on full display as she bamboozled some of the world's finest batters, including the dangerous Meg Lanning. Reflecting on this occasion, Sophie subsequently observed, "'The Ashes is where you're really tested. You're up against the best, and I've always relished that challenge'" (BBC Sport). Her ability to rise to the occasion during such a key series showed the world that Sophie was not only a youthful talent but a player who could be relied upon in tight situations.

As the series went, Sophie continued to demonstrate her significance to the England team. One of her most memorable performances came in the 2021-22 Ashes series, played in Australia. In a key T20 match at Adelaide, Sophie flipped the game on its head with a magnificent bowling display, taking three crucial wickets and restricting Australia to a chaseable total. Her precision and tactical approach to each batter were hailed by observers, who remarked how she had evolved into a world-class bowler capable of winning matches on her own. "'Sophie is the kind of bowler you want in any Ashes match,'" former England captain Charlotte Edwards commented. "'She has this amazing ability to sense the moment and deliver exactly what the team needs'" (The Guardian).

Another key moment came during the multi-format 2021-22 Ashes Test match in Canberra, where

Sophie once again stepped up in a high-pressure scenario. In the fourth inning, with Australia chasing down a tough target and the game hanging in the balance, Sophie bowled with remarkable control, ensuring that England hung on for a hard-fought draw. Her ability to retain her nerve and bowl tight, uncompromising overs at vital moments was a testament to her growing maturity as a player. After the match, Sophie acknowledged the intensity of the fight, stating, "'Every Ashes Test has these big moments, and as a team, we thrive on that. We live for the battle'" (Sky Sports). It's apparent that the Ashes have offered Sophie some of her greatest challenges and have helped her evolve into one of the most formidable spinners in the world.

Beyond her individual accomplishments, Sophie's leadership on the field has also emerged as a distinguishing part of her Ashes career. As she gained more experience, she began playing a more vocal part in steering the team's bowling strategy, often observed talking with the captain and expressing suggestions on field placements. Her grasp of the game, along with her ability to outthink hitters, has made her a vital asset, particularly in Ashes matches where every instant may sway the flow of the series. Her captain Heather Knight once noted Sophie's growing influence, saying, "'Sophie is not just a bowler for us anymore. She's a leader out there, and the way she reads the game is fantastic. In the Ashes, having someone like that is priceless. (The Telegraph).

The Ashes series is more than simply another challenge for Sophie Ecclestone; it is where she has constantly demonstrated her capacity to compete under enormous pressure and produce when it matters most. These defining moments—whether it's getting key wickets, keeping Australia's world-class batsmen in check, or stepping up as a leader—have reinforced her position as one of the most prominent players in women's cricket. For young cricketers watching Sophie in the Ashes, she epitomizes what it means to not just rise to the occasion but also relish the challenge of confronting the greatest in the world.

Sophie Ecclestone's Ashes trip is far from over. With each series, she continues to write new chapters in her incredible career, leaving an unforgettable stamp on one of the sport's greatest rivalries. As the fights between England and Australia continue, one thing is certain: Sophie will be at the heart of England's efforts, producing pivotal moments that will impact the future of the Women's Ashes for years to come.

6.2. World Cup Appearances and Heroics

Sophie Ecclestone's emergence on the world scene has been nothing short of amazing, with her World Cup performances confirming her position as one of the finest spin spinners in women's cricket. Competing in numerous ICC Women's T20 World Cups and ODI World Cups, Sophie has played vital roles in helping England challenge the top teams in the world, providing remarkable performances that have both saved and won crucial matches for her country. Her journey in these worldwide games has been defined by both individual brilliance and the pain of near-misses, but through it all, Sophie's exploits have made her an integral part of England's cricketing legacy.

2017 ICC Women's Cricket World Cup: The Breakthrough

Sophie Ecclestone's first major World Cup appearance occurred in the 2017 ICC Women's Cricket World Cup, held in England. At the age of just 18, she was one of the youngest participants in the tournament, yet she bowled with the composure and poise of a seasoned veteran. Despite her minimal international experience, Sophie was important to England's bowling strategy throughout the competition. In the group stages, she put in impressive performances against teams like South

Africa and New Zealand, holding her nerve in high-pressure situations.

One of her standout performances came during England's semi-final encounter against South Africa, where she bowled with amazing control. Although she didn't take the most wickets in that match, her performance helped reduce South Africa's batting, allowing England to chase the target. England went on to win the match by just two wickets in a dramatic conclusion. This victory set up a historic final at Lord's, where England faced India. Although Sophie did not play in the final match itself, her performances throughout the tournament helped England win their fourth World Cup. Reflecting on her maiden World Cup experience, Sophie subsequently stated, "'It was incredible to be part of a team that won a World Cup on home soil. Just being in that environment at such a young age showed me what it needed to succeed at the highest level." (BBC Sport).

2018 ICC Women's T20 World Cup:: Rising Star

Sophie's second major tournament appearance came in the 2018 ICC Women's T20 World Cup in the West Indies. By this time, Sophie had already established herself as England's go-to spinner, and the expectations were higher than ever. The T20 format, with its emphasis on aggressive, fast-paced cricket, was the perfect stage for Sophie to display her talents. In the group stages, she showed solid performances, taking wickets at vital periods.

England's match versus South Africa in the group stages was a monument to Sophie's ability to manage the game. With South Africa chasing a modest total, Sophie bowled a fantastic spell, getting 2 for 22 in her four overs. Her precision and cunning use of flight forced the South African batters into errors, resulting in their collapse and ensuring England's place in the semi-finals.

In the semi-final versus India, Sophie played a significant role in restraining the Indian hitters. Her stats of 2 for 22 helped England reduce India to just 112, a total England took down with ease. However, in the final, England faced a talented Australian squad that proved too strong. Despite Sophie's best efforts, Australia strolled to an eight-wicket victory, but Sophie's achievements throughout the tournament garnered her significant accolades. Speaking about her progress as a player, she stated, "'The T20 World Cup was where I really felt like I belonged. Every game seemed like a struggle, but I relished the pressure of being the one the team counted on to create a breakthrough." (Sky Sports).

2020 ICC Women's T20 World Cup: The Heartbreak

The 2020 ICC Women's T20 World Cup in Australia was another opportunity for Sophie to demonstrate her world-class abilities on the largest stage. England began the tournament with great aspirations, and Sophie was supposed to be a significant character. Throughout the group stages, she provided strong performances, taking wickets consistently and often bowling in the most difficult conditions.

One of Sophie's best performances came in England's group stage encounter against the West Indies, where she took 3 for 7 in a devastating spell that utterly demolished the Windies' middle order. England's score of 143 was too much for the West Indies, largely because of Sophie's heroics with the ball, which helped secure a 46-run victory.

However, the semi-final against India would prove to be a big heartbreak for both Sophie and England. In a tragic twist of fate, torrential rain washed out the semi-final without a ball being bowled, and India went to the final based on their higher group stage rating. Sophie, who had been in excellent shape throughout the tournament, was left devastated. Speaking to the reporters later, she remarked, "'It's hard to accept. We were ready for a fight, but sometimes things are out of your control. We'll come back stronger." (The Independent). Despite the disappointment, Sophie's efforts had once again established her as one of the elite bowlers in the world.

2022 ICC Women's Cricket World Cup: The Redemption

Sophie's trip to the 2022 ICC Women's Cricket World Cup in New Zealand was a testament to her player improvement. England came into the competition with high hopes of recovering the title, and Sophie's contributions were once again essential. Throughout the competition, Sophie was England's top performer, collecting 21 wickets in nine matches—the highest by any bowler in the tournament.

One of her defining performances came in the semi-final against South Africa, where Sophie took 6 for 36, her best ODI stats to date. Her stunning spell broke the back of the South African batting lineup, sealing England's spot in the final. However, England faced a determined Australian squad in the final, and despite Sophie's best efforts, including taking two wickets, Australia proved too strong, recording a magnificent score of 356. England's chase collapsed, and Australia triumphed by 71 runs.

Despite the setback, Sophie's accomplishments throughout the tournament won her the accolade of being named in the ICC Team of the Tournament. Reflecting on her World Cup adventure, Sophie commented, "'You always want to win the World Cup, but to be able to contribute like I did was special. It's why we play the game—to be part of these moments." (ESPNcricinfo).

Sophie Ecclestone's World Cup appearances have been distinguished by moments of brilliance, resilience, and sadness. Her participation in these global events has confirmed her place among the world's top bowlers and continues to inspire cricketers around the world.

6.3. Memorable matches and turning points

Sophie Ecclestone's journey to fame in international cricket has been punctuated by several memorable matches and critical turning points that not only define her career but also illustrate her influence on the game. From amazing individual displays to match-winning spells, Sophie has constantly delivered in high-pressure situations. These matches are more than just landmarks in her career—they reflect her progress as a player, her capacity to adapt and improve, and the way she has affected the outcomes of some of cricket's biggest championships.

1. England vs. Australia, 2019 Ashes Test at Taunton: A Defining Spell:

One of the most memorable matches in Sophie Ecclestone's career came during the 2019 Women's Ashes, where she announced herself as a significant player in one of the most famous rivalries in cricket. England were under enormous pressure in the only Test of the series, held at Taunton, with Australia putting on a dominant effort. With a formidable Australian batting team containing the likes of Meg Lanning and Ellyse Perry, the odds were firmly stacked against England.

In the first inning, Sophie bowled a superb spell, taking 3 for 74, eliminating key batsmen like Alyssa Healy and Ellyse Perry. Her crisp lines and flighty deliveries prevented the Australians from running away with the game. Although the match ended in a draw, Sophie's effort was vital in preventing

Australia from getting a complete stranglehold over the contest. It was this performance that defined her as a real force in Test cricket, and critics recognized her ability to thrive under the particular strains of the longest format of the game. Sophie herself reflected on the event, saying, "'That match taught me so much about Test cricket. You have to be patient, and sometimes it's about doing your job over lengthy spells rather than just taking wickets." (The Guardian).

2. England vs. West Indies, 2020 ICC Women's T20 World Cup—AA Game-Changing Spell:
The 2020 ICC Women's T20 World Cup in Australia featured one of Sophie's most remarkable T20 performances. England met the West Indies in a critical group stage match, with a semi-final position on the line. The West Indies were known for their potent batting lineup, and England needed to restrict them to ensure a place in the knockouts.

Sophie delivered one of the event's highlight spells, taking 3 for 7 in her four overs. She single-handedly demolished the West Indies' middle order, using her variations to outfox experienced batsmen like Stafanie Taylor and Deandra Dottin. England went on to win the match by 46 runs, and Sophie's performance was acclaimed as a masterclass in spin bowling in T20 cricket. Her ability to deliver under duress was again on full display, and her economy rate of 1.75 was a credit to her control and precision. After the game, Sophie stated, "'T20 cricket is all about holding your nerve. You can't get upset when a hitter is attempting to hit you out of the park, and today I just focused on adhering to my plans'" (BBC Sport).

3. England vs. South Africa, 2022 ICC Women's Cricket World Cup Semi-Final—CCareer-Best Figures:

One of the most critical turning points in Sophie's career happened during the 2022 ICC Women's Cricket World Cup in New Zealand. England played

South Africa in the semi-final, and the stakes couldn't have been higher. England were keen to reach the final following a mixed group stage, and Sophie delivered a career-best performance that sealed her team's spot in the championship match.

Sophie's 6 for 36 against South Africa was not just her greatest ODI stats but also one of the most dominant bowling displays in World Cup history. She decimated South Africa's batting order, removing crucial players like Laura Wolvaardt and Mignon du Preez. Her ability to take wickets at vital stages hindered South Africa from developing partnerships, and they were bowled out for 156, a score England chased down convincingly. Sophie's spell was acclaimed as a match-winning performance, and she was selected Player of the Match. Reflecting on the game, she stated, "'It was one of those days where everything just clicked. The pressure was immense, but I trusted myself to keep attacking and create the breakthroughs we needed." (ESPNcricinfo).

4. England vs. India, 2021 Multi-Format Series: The Battle in Bristol

In the summer of 2021, England hosted India in a multi-format series that included one Test, three ODIs, and three T20s. The first match, a one-off Test at Bristol, was another turning point for Sophie. In a dramatic, hard-fought draw, Sophie's bowling was once again essential to England's efforts to control the game.

In the second innings, India were chasing a target of 231 runs when Sophie bowled a marathon stint of 38 overs, taking 4 for 88. Her patience and skill were essential in keeping India at bay as they threatened to track down the target. The match ended in a draw, but Sophie's performance was greatly recognized for her endurance and tactical genius. Former England captain Charlotte Edwards observed, "'Sophie bowled her heart out in that Test.

Her control and stamina were incredible—she's becoming one of the best bowlers in the world, across all formats'" (The Telegraph).

5. England vs. Australia, 2022 Women's Ashes—T20 Heroics in Adelaide:

The 2022 Women's Ashes, played in Australia, featured one of Sophie's defining performances in the T20 format. In a must-win encounter in Adelaide, Sophie once again rose to the occasion, taking 3 for 15 to lead England to victory. Australia, known for their aggressive T20 batting, were reduced to 119 for 9, primarily owing to Sophie's tight bowling. She dismissed Meg Lanning, Tahlia McGrath, and Rachael Haynes, all of whom were vital to Australia's batting depth.

Sophie's ability to deliver in big circumstances was on full display as she outwitted some of the top T20 batsmen in the world. England chased down the target with ease, and Sophie's spell was acknowledged as the turning point in the contest.

After the game, she observed, "'T20 is fast, and you have to adapt quickly. I knew I had to take out their main players, and it worked. It's one of those games I'll never forget'" (Sky Sports).

Sophie Ecclestone's career is packed with spectacular matches and turning occasions, but what makes her truly exceptional is her ability to constantly produce in high-stakes circumstances. Whether it's an Ashes Test, a World Cup semi-final, or a key T20 encounter, Sophie has demonstrated time and again that she is one of the most reliable and effective bowlers in women's cricket. These performances not only characterize her as a player, but also demonstrate her ability to change the course of a match through sheer skill and drive.

CHAPTER 7

OFF THE FIELD: PERSONALITY AND PHILOSOPHY

7.1. The Role Model: Sophie's Influence Beyond the Game

Sophie Ecclestone's brilliance on the cricket pitch is only one part of her narrative. Beyond her exploits in the sport, Sophie has built out a reputation as a role model and inspiration to innumerable young cricketers and fans worldwide. Her off-the-field nature, combined with her approachability, modesty, and devotion to giving back, has reinforced her status as a beacon of hope and a positive effect beyond the borders of cricket.

From the outset of her career, Sophie has always embodied a down-to-earth, relatable attitude that sets her apart from many sports. Despite her swift rise to becoming one of the world's top bowlers, Sophie has remained grounded, never letting success inflate her ego. Whether she's talking with followers on social media, giving interviews, or participating in community activities, Sophie's honesty and generosity always shine through. She once remarked in an interview, "'I've always wanted to stay true to who I am. Cricket's been a significant part of my life, but it's vital to remember where you came from and the people who helped you along the way'" (The Independent).

This attitude of humility is one of the reasons why so many young cricketers look up to Sophie as a role model. For many, she represents the idea that hard work, devotion, and a genuine love for the game can carry you to the highest levels. Sophie often lectures on the significance of mental resilience and perseverance, particularly for aspiring female athletes who face unique hurdles in a historically male-dominated sport. Her message is clear: cricket—and any sport—should be a venue where women feel inspired to excel, regardless of the challenges.

One of the most significant aspects of Sophie's influence beyond the game is her support for women's cricket and gender equality in sports. As the prominence of women's cricket continues to expand, Sophie has utilized her position to press for improved recognition, resources, and opportunities for female cricketers. In interviews and public appearances, Sophie often acknowledges the progress that has been accomplished but stresses that there is still more to be done. Speaking about the increased prominence of women's cricket, she added, "'We're at an exciting time for women's cricket, but we can't stop here. It's about making sure the next generation has even better possibilities than we did." (BBC Sport). Her zeal for improving the women's game is clear, and her advocacy is encouraging not just to new players but also to spectators who regard her as a pioneer in the drive for gender equality.

Beyond cricket, Sophie's humanitarian activities clearly display her deep commitment to making a difference. She is actively involved in several humanitarian efforts, notably those focused on youth development and mental health awareness. Having faced the challenges of being a young athlete on the international stage, Sophie has spoken freely about the significance of mental health support in athletics. She is a firm believer in establishing a supportive atmosphere for young athletes, ensuring they have the resources and advice to cope with the emotional demands of professional sports. In conjunction with mental health groups, Sophie has worked to increase awareness about these concerns, encouraging open talks and destigmatizing mental health struggles.

Her involvement in community service also extends to grassroots cricket. Sophie often participates in coaching clinics, particularly in poor regions, where she shares her experience and passion for the game with young players who may not have access to top-tier coaching. Her participation in these settings is more than just symbolic; she is actively hands-on, encouraging and guiding the next generation. In a wonderful moment during one of these clinics, a young girl from a local club said, "'Meeting Sophie made me believe that I can make it too. She's not simply a cricketer; she's someone who cares about us and wants to help us grow'" (Sky Sports).

Sophie's impact off the field also extends to her role as an ambassador for many brands and campaigns advocating positive change. She is associated with efforts that promote sustainability, diversity, and inclusion, using her influence to expose key social concerns. Her collaboration with these causes reflects her idea that athletes can be strong agents of change, not just within their sport but in society as a whole.

Ultimately, Sophie Ecclestone's effect extends beyond the game to her ability to connect with people. Whether it's via her humanitarian efforts, her advocacy for women's cricket, or her down-to-earth nature, Sophie has become a role model who epitomizes much more than her on-field successes. She helps us remember that success is about using your platform to inspire and motivate others. As her career grows, Sophie's effect will definitely continue to resonate, not just as a cricketer but as a leader and champion for positive change around the globe.

7.2. Philanthropy and community work

While Sophie Ecclestone's skill on the cricket field is well-known, her accomplishments off the field, via philanthropy and community engagement, have equally reinforced her standing as a true role model. Sophie's devotion to make a difference in the lives of others extends beyond the confines of athletics, as she actively works in humanitarian activities, youth development programs, and raising awareness around key social concerns. Through her philanthropic and community initiatives, Sophie has proved that her influence stretches far beyond cricket, and her genuine desire to give back has created a lasting impact on the communities she affects.

Sophie's charity career began as her status in international cricket grew. Understanding the platform that cricket had provided her, she was resolved to use it for the greater good. Much of her humanitarian work is centered on her enthusiasm for supporting young people, particularly girls, to pursue their dreams, despite the hurdles they may face. A frequent participant in youth coaching clinics and school visits, Sophie often dedicates time to grassroots cricket, where she can inspire the next generation of players. By describing her personal path from a young girl playing in local clubs to becoming the world's top-ranked bowler,

Sophie encourages young athletes to realize that success is feasible with hard effort and devotion.

One of the notable characteristics of Sophie's community work is her focus on giving opportunities to individuals who may not have access to the same resources. Through her work with initiatives like the Chance to Shine program, a nonprofit focused on promoting cricket in state schools and underprivileged regions across the UK, Sophie has been at the forefront of efforts to ensure that cricket is accessible to all. She has spent time coaching youngsters from impoverished homes, emphasizing the value of inclusion and representation in athletics. After a session with Chance to Shine, Sophie commented, "'I want every child, no matter where they come from, to have the chance to play cricket and to know that the sky's the limit. Seeing the delight in their faces when they get to play makes it all worthwhile." (Sky Sports). Her hands-on involvement in these programs shows her commitment to breaking down barriers and ensuring that cricket is a sport for everyone, regardless of socioeconomic background.

Sophie's philanthropic reach extends beyond sports. She has been a passionate champion for mental health awareness, particularly among young athletes. Recognizing the challenges that come with competing at the highest levels, Sophie has teamed with numerous mental health groups to raise awareness about the importance of mental well-being in sport. In 2021-22, she collaborated with 'Mind', a mental health charity in the UK, to design ads that inspire athletes to seek treatment and speak honestly about their mental health difficulties. Sophie has expressed her personal experiences with the pressures of international cricket, emphasizing that it's okay to feel overwhelmed and seek support. Speaking on the significance of mental health, she stated, "'As athletes, we're often expected to be tough all the time, but we're human. Mental health is equally as essential as physical health, and it's appropriate to seek help.(BBC Sport).

Another key component of Sophie's community work is her commitment to promoting sustainability and environmental awareness. As part of her association with numerous eco-conscious firms, Sophie has been an advocate for making cricket more environmentally sustainable. She has voiced her support for efforts aimed at reducing waste in sports arenas and encouraging spectators to be more mindful of their environmental impact. This component of her generosity highlights Sophie's willingness to use her position to solve global challenges that transcend athletics.

Sophie's passion for philanthropy is especially obvious in her support of women's empowerment initiatives. She has actively pushed for gender equality in sport, working with groups like the 'Women in Sport' foundation to promote equal opportunities for women and girls in athletics. Sophie has been a significant voice in asking for improved financing and attention for women's cricket, and she has underlined the necessity of having an equal playing field for female players through her advocacy. "'We've made so much progress in women's cricket, but we can't stop here. "We need to keep striving for equality in all sports for every girl out there who dreams of being a professional athlete," Sophie stated in a speech at a women's sports event (The Telegraph).

At the center of Sophie Ecclestone's philanthropy and community engagement is her belief that sport has the potential to alter lives. Whether it's providing children the chance to pick up a bat for the first time, fighting for mental health assistance in sports, or lobbying for gender equality, Sophie's actions illustrate her commitment to utilize her success for the sake of others. Her influence off the field is a mirror of her character—kind, caring, and profoundly driven to making the world a better place for future generations. As Sophie continues to shatter barriers in cricket, her humanitarian legacy is only going to increase, leaving an everlasting imprint on the lives she affects both on and off the field.

7.3. Balancing Life as a Professional Athlete

For Sophie Ecclestone, juggling the demands of life as a professional athlete is a continual challenge, one that involves discipline, focus, and a constant reevaluation of priorities. Being one of the top bowlers in women's cricket comes with great expectations—not only to succeed on the field, but also to manage the off-field duties that come with celebrity and success. Yet, Sophie has managed to keep a grounded approach to life, continually seeking to achieve the perfect balance between her cricketing career and her personal life.

Sophie's experience as a professional athlete started when she was still a teenager, and from an early age, she had to learn how to handle the pressures of international cricket while managing the intricacies of growing up in the public eye. The arduous pace of international cricket—filled with tours, training camps, and media obligations—can often be daunting for sportsmen. For Sophie, keeping a balance between her professional duties and home life has been crucial to her well-being and long-term success. She once observed, "'Being a professional cricketer is an amazing job, but it's also relentless at times. You're always on the move, and it's crucial to find time for yourself to switch off from the game." (BBC Sport).

Sophie's excellent support system is one of the most important parts of her approach to balancing her life as an athlete. Family and friends play a vital role in keeping her grounded and giving her a feeling of normalcy among the continual frenzy of professional athletics. Sophie is often frank about the value of having people around her who help her keep connected to her roots and who provide emotional support during the tough moments of her career. She constantly talks about how her family's unshakable support has been a constant source of strength, noting, "My family has always been my anchor." They remind me that there's more to life than cricket, and that perspective is so vital, especially when things go tough" (The Independent).

Another crucial part of Sophie's life balance is her mental health. In a sport as demanding as cricket, where competitors are often away from home for extended periods, the mental toll can be enormous. Sophie has been outspoken about the necessity of taking care of her mental well-being, especially as the expectations of professional athletics begin to mount. She emphasizes the necessity for professional athletes to identify when they need a break or help, noting, "'There's nothing wrong with needing a break from cricket or from any sport. Taking time to refresh psychologically is equally as vital as any physical training session'" (Sky Sports). For Sophie, this means finding relaxation times where she can completely detach from cricket, whether through spending time with loved ones, participating in hobbies, or simply having time to rest.

Maintaining physical health is, of course, another concern for any professional athlete, and Sophie recognizes the necessity of maintaining her body in optimum shape to meet the demands of international cricket. Rigorous training schedules and matches can take a toll, and Sophie has created a strong routine of recovery and self-care to ensure that she can sustain a long and successful career. Whether through training regimes, a good diet, or regular relaxation, Sophie is committed to the holistic care of her body to avoid injury and stay at the top of her game.

In the end, balancing life as a professional athlete is about handling the varied demands of sport, celebrity, and personal well-being. For Sophie Ecclestone, this balance is something she continuously works on, learning to combine the obligations of being one of the world's top cricketers while remaining connected to her personal values and relationships. It's a delicate balancing act, but one that Sophie embraces with humility and elegance, recognizing that the secret to success rests not just in winning on the field but also in maintaining a healthy, full life off it.

CHAPTER 8
FUTURE ASPIRATIONS AND LEGACY

8.1. Goals for the Future

As Sophie Ecclestone continues to rise through the ranks of international cricket, her emphasis on future objectives remains clear and ambitious. Already considered one of the top spin bowlers in the world, Sophie's future aims are not only about boosting her personal successes but also about contributing to the larger evolution of women's cricket. With her unshakable dedication, competitive attitude, and profound love for the game, Sophie is motivated to build on her triumphs and create a lasting legacy that extends beyond numbers.

One of Sophie's most immediate aims is to preserve her place as a world-class spinner across all versions of the game. While she is now considered among the top bowlers in both T20 and ODI cricket, Sophie is continually pushing herself to be better. In interviews, she has repeatedly emphasized her ambition to enhance her game by adding new variations to her bowling, honing her techniques, and continuing to challenge the finest batters in the world. ' "There's always something to improve in cricket,'" Sophie stated in an interview with 'ESPNcricinfo'. "'I never want to get too comfortable. Whether it's adding a new delivery or improving my consistency, I'm always working on anything to push my game to the next level." ' This relentless drive for improvement is a hallmark of Sophie's career and a key part of her future aspirations.

A significant goal that remains on Sophie's mind is winning additional World Cups with England. While she has previously played crucial roles in multiple ICC tournaments, including the 2017 World Cup success and her spectacular performance in the 2022 Women's Cricket World Cup, Sophie has voiced a genuine desire to continue adding to her World Cup total. For Sophie, winning a World Cup is not only about personal glory—it's about the pride of representing her country and contributing to the evolution of women's cricket on the global stage. She has made it plain that the ultimate goal is to help England become the most dominant power in women's cricket, and winning another World Cup would be a major part of that mission. "'There's nothing like the feeling of lifting a World Cup with your teammates,'" Sophie once stated. "'But we want to keep winning and keep pushing to be the best team in the world.'"

Sophie is also intent on securing her legacy in Test cricket, a sport she regards highly beyond World Cups. Though women's Test matches are less common, Sophie is enthusiastic about playing more Tests and becoming a prominent player in the future of women's red-ball cricket. She has expressed her desire to play more multi-day matches and help reignite the popularity of women's Test cricket. In her words, "'Test cricket is the ultimate test of a player's skill and mental toughness. I want to play as many Tests as possible and show that women's Test cricket can be just as thrilling and competitive as the men's game'" (The Telegraph). This aim echoes Sophie's greater goal of promoting the women's game and ensuring it receives the recognition it deserves across all formats.

Sophie's role as a leader within the England squad is another crucial component of her future goals. Sophie, who is not yet captain, has started taking on more on-field and off-field duties. As she continues to mature, there is a strong likelihood that Sophie might take up a formal leadership role within the squad, whether as a vice captain or eventually as captain. She has acknowledged her appreciation for current captain Heather Knight and former England captains, stating, "'I've learned so much from

Heather and other senior players. Leadership is something that's incredibly important to me, and I hope to be someone that younger players can look forward to'" (BBC Sport). As Sophie evolves into a leadership position, she will likely continue to mentor younger players and help push England into the next age of women's cricket.

Off the field, Sophie's aspirations are just as lofty. She has spoken freely about her ambition to be involved in coaching and mentoring once her playing days are done. Sophie has a keen interest in working with young players and passing on the knowledge and experience she has garnered over her career. In particular, she wants to guarantee that young girls who dream of playing cricket get the resources and support they need to succeed. ' "When I was growing up, I didn't always have female cricketers to look up to,'" Sophie stated in an interview with 'Sky Sports'. "'I want to be that role model for the next generation and help them believe they can achieve anything they set their minds to." '

Whether through coaching, mentoring, or involvement in youth development programs, Sophie's long-term goal is to contribute to the growth of women's cricket at the grassroots level.

Sophie's future objectives are strongly connected with her desire to leave a lasting legacy—not just as one of the best bowlers in the history of women's cricket, but as someone who played a vital role in the sport's progression. Her aims show a commitment to personal greatness, team success, and the larger development of women's cricket. As Sophie looks ahead, there's no doubt that she will continue to break barriers, inspire future generations, and affect the future of the game she loves.

8.2. Sophie's Vision for Women's Cricket

Sophie Ecclestone, already acknowledged as one of the most prominent figures in women's cricket, is far from finished. At the height of her career, she carries not only the expectations of her team but the hope of an entire generation of young women eager to forge their own way in cricket. Her goals, both for herself and for the future of the game, demonstrate a deep understanding of the platform she wields and the responsibility that comes with it. In interviews and public declarations, Sophie has repeatedly voiced her ambition not simply to be recognized as a brilliant player but as someone who helped reshape the landscape of women's cricket for the future generation.

Sophie's vision for the future of sport extends beyond the cricket field in many ways. She wants to see women's cricket attain the kind of mainstream acceptance and respect that men's cricket has long had, both in terms of media attention and financial backing. "The game has grown massively, and I'm proud to have been part of that, but we can't stop here," she remarked in an interview with 'The Guardian'. "We need to keep pushing for more opportunities, more investment, and better facilities for girls and women coming into the sport."

For Sophie, it's not just about providing women the chance to play; it's about giving them the resources to excel. She sees a world where young females have the same degree of access to training, coaching, and competitive opportunities as their male peers. This implies stronger financial support for grassroots initiatives, better visibility through media coverage, and more professional leagues that can provide long-term career prospects for women cricketers. "There's so much talent out there," she remarked. "We need to nurture it and create a system where girls can dream of becoming professional cricketers from a young age without feeling like they're fighting against the odds."

Sophie's vision is also about representation. She appreciates the value of having visible role models for young girls who are just beginning to show an interest in sports. When she looks back on her early years, Sophie often mentions how few female cricketers were consistently visible in the media, and how this affected her own sense of what was possible. "When I was young, you didn't see women cricketers on TV that much," she stated in a BBC Sport interview. "Now, young girls can turn on the television and watch women's cricket, and that's massive. That's where it all starts—with visibility." She hopes that in the future, the media will provide more consistent coverage of women's cricket, not just during World Cups or major tournaments, but throughout the year, allowing young fans to grow up following their heroes as they do in men's cricket.

A major element of Sophie's legacy will be how she advocates inclusion in cricket. She has spoken multiple times on the need for cricket to reach a bigger, more diversified audience. "Cricket should be a sport for everyone, no matter where you come from or what background you have," she told 'Sky Sports'. "We need to make sure that we're getting the message out there that cricket is for everyone and that there are pathways for everyone, no matter who you are."

For Sophie, the struggle for inclusivity extends to every area of the sport—ensuring that young women from underprivileged backgrounds can access the same opportunities and that girls from all communities feel welcomed in cricket clubs across the country. She wants to see cricket break out of the image of exclusivity and become a truly universal sport, where the passion for the game knows no limits.

On the field, Sophie is pushed by her desire to continue improving. Although she's already a fixture in the record books, she doesn't see herself resting on her laurels anytime soon. Her own objectives are strongly related to the aims of the teams she plays for—England, obviously, but also the women's clubs she represents in various divisions. "I want to keep getting better, to push myself and see how far I can go," she once told 'Cricbuzz'. "There's always room to improve, and there's always another challenge around the corner."

However, despite the personal accolades, Sophie's objective is clear: leaving the game in a better place than she found it. She wants her legacy to be about more than wickets and records; she wants it to be about the opportunities she helped open for others. "I'd love to be remembered as someone who made a difference, not just on the pitch but off it," she told 'The Times'. "It's about making sure that when I leave the game, girls coming through have more opportunities than I did."

In the years to come, Sophie Ecclestone's name will certainly be synonymous with success on the cricket field, but maybe her greatest memorable legacy will be her unflinching devotion to growing the sport for future generations. Her vision for women's cricket is bold, inclusive, and constantly forward-thinking—a reflection of her personal path and the principles she bears as a role model for aspiring cricketers everywhere. Through her leadership, both on and off the field, Sophie is motivated to help shatter new barriers, ensuring that the future of women's cricket is brighter, more accessible, and full of infinite promise.

8.3. Building a Lasting Legacy

For Sophie Ecclestone, the concept of legacy goes far beyond personal achievements and records. While she is already acknowledged as one of the most accomplished cricketers of her time, her goals extend to how she can change the future of women's cricket and inspire a new wave of talent. Building a lasting legacy is about more than just her numbers on the field—it's about how she can affect the sport long after she's bowled her last delivery.

In her own words, Sophie has often thought about the responsibility that comes with accomplishment. "I've been lucky to have a platform, but it's about what you do with that platform that counts," she remarked in an interview with 'The Telegraph'. "I don't just want to be remembered for my performances; I want to be remembered for helping the game grow." This statement reflects her idea that greatness in sport isn't just about individual milestones but about the greater impact one has on the game and its community.

A fundamental component of Sophie's legacy will be how she has revolutionized what's possible for women in cricket. Having debuted for England at such an early age and swiftly establishing herself as one of the world's leading spinners, she has become an example of how ability, commitment, and enthusiasm can transcend obstacles. Her ascent to fame has shattered many old notions of women's cricket, showing that it is feasible for female cricketers to command the same degree of respect and affection as their male counterparts. "I want people to look at women's cricket and not see it as something lesser, but as a sport that stands on its own, with its own heroes and legends," she once told 'The Guardian'.

Sophie's approach to her legacy is intimately tied to the idea of influencing others. She constantly discusses her wish to leave behind a pathway for young girls who dream of playing cricket professionally. "When I was starting out, the opportunities were there, but they weren't as visible," she stated in an interview with 'BBC Sport'. "Now, girls can see us playing on TV, see what we're achieving, and hopefully think, 'I can do that too.' I want to make sure that pathway is not just open but clear for them to follow."

Her efforts in this area go beyond merely being a role model. Sophie has been actively involved in coaching young cricketers, passing on her skills, and helping mold the future generation of players. She has participated in various youth cricket initiatives, donating her time and insights to inspire the next crop of talent. For Sophie, it's crucial that young athletes learn that success doesn't come overnight. "I always tell them it's about working hard every day, even when things aren't going your way. That's what develops a career; that's what builds a legacy," she told 'Cricbuzz'.

Additionally, Sophie has continually advocated for better circumstances for women in cricket. Whether it's via pushing for more fair compensation, improved facilities, or increased visibility for women's matches, Sophie wants to see the sport progress in ways that benefit future generations. "I want to leave the game in a better place than I found it," she once remarked during a news conference. "If girls growing up now have more opportunities and better resources and don't have to fight as hard for recognition, then I'll know I've done my part."

Part of developing a lasting legacy for Sophie is also connected to leadership. As one of the older figures in the England team, she has naturally taken on a leadership role, both in terms of her on-field performances and in the dressing room. Her cool manner under pressure, paired with her tenacious work ethic, has made her a source of inspiration not just to young cricketers, but to her colleagues as well. "She's the kind of player who leads by example," said England captain Heather Knight in a piece by 'Sky Sports'. "She doesn't need to talk a lot—her performances say everything."

Sophie also knows the necessity of having an impact off the field. She has been open about using her platform to support causes that connect with her, particularly in the areas of women's empowerment and mental health in sports. "Being in the public eye gives you a voice, and it's important to use that voice for good," Sophie stated in an interview with 'The Times'. "Cricket has given me so much, and I want to give back—not just to the game, but to the community around it."

As Sophie looks ahead to the future, her aim is clear: she wants to continue pushing boundaries, setting new standards for excellence, and ensuring that the doors she has walked through stay wide open for those who follow after her. While her personal ambitions—such as winning more World Cups and dominating in more Ashes series—remain high, she is equally devoted to crafting a future where women's cricket is more accessible, more inclusive, and more celebrated.

In the years to come, Sophie Ecclestone's legacy will likely be defined not just by the wickets she's taken or the records she's broken, but by the effect she has made in the lives of young girls who strive to be just like her. Her lasting legacy will be the future she helps build—a future where women's cricket thrives, where chances are numerous, and where talent is cultivated and appreciated regardless of gender. In Sophie's own words, "That's the legacy I want to leave behind—one where the game is better for having had me in it."

APPENDICES

CAREER STATISTICS AND RECORDS

Sophie Ecclestone's cricketing career is distinguished by a steady, almost unbreakable dominance that has altered the role of spin bowling in women's cricket. From the moment she broke into the England squad as a teenager, her journey to the top has been nothing short of spectacular. With every match, she adds new chapters to her already amazing record, solidifying her place among the all-time greats of the game.

When we look at Sophie's statistics, the figures reveal a story of both skill and longevity. As of 2023, she has played over 80 One Day Internationals (ODIs) and more than 70 T20

Internationals (T20Is) for England, with match-winning performances across both forms. With an economy rate regularly under four runs per over in ODIs and an exceptional average of just over 20 in both forms, Sophie's bowling is a credit to her precision, control, and ability to adjust to varied conditions. Her T20 economy rate, which is extremely low, makes her one of the most difficult bowlers to score against in the shortest format.

Her wicket tally is undoubtedly the most defining feature of her career. Sophie has always been one of the top wicket-takers in ODIs, with her name frequently appearing in the upper echelons of the ICC rankings. By the age of 23, she had already crossed the 100-wicket mark in ODIs, an amazing record for a spinner in modern cricket. Her ability to bowl inexpensively while consistently getting wickets has earned her England's go-to bowler in pressure circumstances. In fact, her career-best stats of 6 for 36 against South Africa in the 2022 Women's Cricket World Cup are a testament to her match-winning prowess in high-stakes confrontations. That performance not only helped her team advance but also confirmed her reputation as one of the most reliable bowlers in world cricket.

Sophie's record in T20 internationals is as impressive. Known for her precision and innovative variations, she has become one of the most effective bowlers in the format. Her T20 career includes multiple five-wicket hauls, and she was important in England's march to the 2020 ICC Women's T20 World Cup final. Her ability to bowl in both the powerplay and death overs shows her flexibility. She is trusted to bowl in the most trying parts of the game, which is a credit to her maturity and cricketing intelligence.

It's not only the volume of wickets that characterizes Sophie's career; it's her consistency and impact on games. Her ability to deliver under duress has led to multiple Player of the Match accolades. Sophie has also often been at the top of the ICC Women's Player Rankings, earning recognition as the number one-ranked T20 bowler in the world—a status she has held for a long period. Her reign at the top of the rankings is symptomatic of her dominance in the shortest format, and she has constantly upped the bar with each passing year.

In Test cricket, Sophie has also made a huge effect despite the restricted number of matches. Her greatest Test numbers of 8 wickets for 206 runs in a single match against India during the 2021 series showed that she is not only a limited-overs specialist but can also adapt her style to the longer format. With an average of under 30 in Tests, she has proven herself capable of sustaining pressure over extended periods, which is a critical talent in the more traditional form of the game.

Beyond the numbers, Sophie's influence on the game has been tremendous. She has been part of a transformative age in women's cricket, where the sport has acquired unparalleled attention and support. Her contributions have been important to England's success in major events, notably the ICC Women's Cricket World Cup and the Women's Ashes series. Her performances in these legendary games have frequently been vital, shifting the tide of matches and series in England's favor. Her five-wicket haul in the 2021 Ashes T20 was important in sealing a dramatic win for England, further cementing her reputation as a clutch performer.

In addition to her international career, Sophie has been a significant player in domestic tournaments, notably The Hundred and the Women's Big Bash League (WBBL), where she has represented numerous franchises. Her domestic records are similarly spectacular, with standout performances that have earned her a fan favorite around the globe. Whether playing for Manchester Originals in The Hundred or Sydney Sixers in the WBBL, she continues to flourish, demonstrating her skills on the highest stages in domestic cricket.

As Sophie Ecclestone's career continues to unfold, the expectation is that her records will only grow more amazing. With many years of cricket yet ahead of her, Sophie's status as one of the finest bowlers in women's cricket history is firmly established, yet she continues to push limits, reaching for even greater heights. The statistics, while impressive, only represent part of her narrative. What they fail to adequately communicate is the overwhelming impact she has had on the field—both in terms of her ability to win games for her side and her role as a standard-bearer for women's cricket globally.

In the years to come, cricket fans will undoubtedly speak of Sophie Ecclestone's career not just in terms of numbers but in terms of how she altered the game, inspired generations of young cricketers, and set new benchmarks for performance.

Printed in Dunstable, United Kingdom